How to Raise Capital:
Preparing and Presenting a Business Plan

How to Raise Capital

Preparing and Presenting a Business Plan

GREGORY I. KRAVITT

Jeffrey E. Grossman
Karl P. Keller
Korak Mitra
Edward A. Raha
Adam E. Robins

DOW JONES-IRWIN Homewood, Illinois 60430

This publication is designed to provide accurate and authoritative information in regard to the subject matter covered. It is sold with the understanding that the publisher is not engaged in rendering legal, accounting, or other professional service. If legal advice or other expert assistance is required, the services of a competent professional person should be sought.

From a Declaration of Principles jointly adopted by a Committee of the American Bar Association and a Committee of Publishers.

ISBN 0-87094-380-4

Library of Congress Catalog Card No. 82-73630

Printed in the United States of America

3 4 5 6 7 8 9 0 BC 1 0 9 8 7 6 5 4

To Sandy with Love

A Special Thanks to
Jennifer L. Jarosz
and
Barbara A. Lux

CONTENTS

ix

INTRODUCTION

How to Raise Capital is a tool that helps the entrepreneur both to raise and preserve capital. This publication is a working document; it focuses on the pragmatic business issues an entrepreneur must address if he/she is to acquire financing.

Without a well-written and well-documented business plan, the individual seeking capital has virtually no chance of raising money. To prepare a business plan, the entrepreneur has only a few options. He/she can spend valuable time and energy studying various "how-to" books on the subject, which speak in general, philosophical terms but do not deal with the mechanics of writing the business plan itself. Another alternative open to the entrepreneur is to hire the expensive services of a professional deal packager with his company's much-needed capital. Or one can use *How to Raise Capital*, which effectively takes the entrepreneur through the entire process of business planning and analysis.

How to Raise Capital is a complete guide to writing a business plan: no prerequisite reading is required. It is written in questionnaire form; this questionnaire format is designed to elicit information specifically required by the prospective investor. If it is given the proper time and effort, the completed document could be substituted for the expensive services of a professional deal packager. Actually, most investors prefer a business plan written by the entrepreneur rather than the sterile product usually provided by a professional.

This book is designed for any aspiring entrepreneur who wants to start or expand his/her own business. It provides the entrepreneur with both a vehicle for raising seed capital and an efficient method of planning the future development of a small company. This book will also help the entrepreneur pinpoint potential problems and significant risks before they develop into crises. Prospective investors should find this publication also useful as a guideline that can be recommended to entrepreneurs who approach them for financing.

Specifically, the *Business Plan* answers the entrepreneur's questions about how to accomplish the following:

RAISE CAPITAL. By focusing an entrepreneur's attention on specific business issues, *How to Raise Capital* will increase the entrepreneur's chances of raising the capital he needs. Because this book is organized in outline form, it flows in the logical order that the prospective investor prefers. An entrepreneur who utilizes the Business Plan and works through it diligently should have a better chance of attracting the attention of a prospective investor swamped with business proposals.

AVOID RISK OR ERROR. Most entrepreneurs have a tendency to deal with problems as they occur. Often these problems can be extremely damaging or even fatal to a business if the entrepreneur has not prepared contingency plans. The Business Plan causes the entrepreneur to focus on high-risk areas. It encourages the development of solutions and alternative contingency plans *before* problems occur. Strategies that are too risky can be evaluated and avoided before resources are committed.

IMPROVE JOB/BUSINESS PERFORMANCE. Management's knowledge of its own company and industry will be greatly enhanced through the use of the Business Plan. The document directs the entrepreneur to examine changes in product technology, market demographics, and operations management, and many other areas. Using our document, the entrepreneur and the company will be better prepared to address problems and obstacles as they are encountered.

AID IN DECISION-MAKING. Besides forcing the entrepreneur to focus on key problems, this document also helps the entrepreneur with long-term planning and directs him/her to consider solutions to potential problems. In addition, the Business Plan points out areas of the business that one might otherwise have overlooked.

TRACKING AND BUDGETING. By preparing a detailed business plan, the entrepreneur has a projected operating standard against which to compare actual performance. Variances indicate the need for closer examination.

AID IN PLANNING FOR NEW PRODUCT DEVELOPMENT AND INTERNAL CREATION OF NEW VENTURES. By focusing the reader's attention on all the major areas essential to the development of a small business, *How to Raise Capital* organizes, stimulates, and structures the new venture planning process.

How to Raise Capital is organized like a workbook. Each section contains a series of questions that, if answered thoroughly, will inform any investor about the quality of the company seeking financing. Not all the questions will be applicable in every situation. Some questions, such as the one that asks for a history of the company's plant utilization (Sec. VIII, 4.), obviously will not be relevant to a start-up operation.

Immediately below most of the questions, the authors have provided definitions of the concepts that these questions address. These definitions will not only help the aspiring entrepreneur answer the questions completely, but will also serve as a general reference about important business terms.

Besides definitions of key terms, most of the questions contain brief comments entitled the *Investor's Perspective*. These Investor's Perspectives were designed to give the reader helpful insight into what information the investor considers valuable—and, more importantly, why the investor considers that information valuable.

Often these Investor's Perspectives describe the ideal criteria that an investor would find attractive. For example, investors look for companies that are unencumbered by lawsuits, that serve sufficiently diversified markets, and whose management has no conflicts of interest. Of course, few, if any, companies can meet all the ideal criteria described in the Investor's Perspectives. Thus a reader should not use the Investor's Perspectives as a guide to telling the investor only what he/she wants to hear. Such an approach to writing a business plan will inevitably distort the facts about a company. Those who invest in entrepreneurial growth companies are shrewd enough to detect any attempt to gloss over the problems and weaknesses of a particular company. You are more likely to acquire financing for your venture if you show the investor what your company's problems are and how you plan to rectify them. The entrepreneur who does not explain those problems and weaknesses will no doubt have the business plan rejected outright.

Although *How to Raise Capital* is presented in an easy-to-follow question and answer format, the document you present to investors should not be simply a series of questions and answers. The format of this book should be used as a tool for gathering and organizing the data to prepare your business plan. With the use of the information you develop from this book's format, we encourage the user to prepare a coherent, flowing narrative around the structure provided. However, you can use the various chapter headings and other organizing divisions in this book to assemble your firm's business plan. To show how this is done, the authors have assembled two business plans structured in much the same way as the working document that comprises most of *How to Raise Capital*.

To make best use of this book, the user should answer all the questions as fully as possible. Of course, not all the questions may apply to your firm's particular situation, and some sections will deserve more extensive answers than others. But before you skip a question, make sure you fully understand why you have done so: an investor will probably want to know why you have avoided that issue. All the information should be accurately presented so that the investor can make a valid assessment of the risks involved and the returns he can anticipate. Explaining potential risks to the investor will not necessarily detract from the marketability of the business plan, but will actually demonstrate that you have thought out the venture well enough to be aware of all potential risks.

Even if your company is already up and running, it is imperative that when you answer these questions, you *support your assertions by using authoritative reference sources wherever possible.* Include supporting documents as appendices to the business plan you submit to investors.

We believe *How to Raise Capital* gives an aspiring entrepreneur all the tools necessary to write a quality business plan. This book not only addresses all the issues that investors think are essential, but also pinpoints the key considerations an entrepreneur must face to make his business grow and prosper. Of course, we can offer no magic formula to help an entrepreneur generate a business plan that immediately attracts investors. *How to Raise Capital* asks the right questions, but only you can provide the answers. And like most ventures, the success of the final product will be only a reflection of the effort put into it.

Part One

Business Planning and Analysis

I. BACKGROUND

A. Overview

Please provide a one- to three-page summary of your business proposal. Include a description of the subject company's products/services, a brief outline of management's qualifications and major accomplishments, the financial and developmental history of the enterprise, the amount of capital required, the purposes for which proceeds will be used, the nature and growth rate of the market for the subject company's products/services, and the identity of the niche in the market that the subject company will serve.

INVESTOR'S PERSPECTIVE

Because of the large volume of business proposals that investors receive, they prefer a short, succinct summary of the major factors involved. To avoid elimination from further consideration, the entrepreneur should devote the time and effort to compose a clear and convincing overview of his/her proposal.

Keep your Overview brief, two or three pages at most. Try to distill the essence of your company—the uniqueness of your product or service—into a few sentences. Use the rest of the Overview to elaborate on your firm's specific qualities. Explain to your investor what makes your venture worthy of financing. Is it the distinctive market you serve that few other companies have exploited? Is it the overwhelming economic justification of your product?

Also, make sure you provide the investor with the basic information listed below. Addresses and phone numbers are obvious pieces of information, but an investor will also want to know less obvious facts, such as your company's previous name and who referred you to the investor.

1. **Date of application:**

2. **Original name of company and subsequent changes:**

3. **Address of home office:**

4. **Phone number:**

5. **Date business was established:**

6. **Name and affiliation of the person who referred you:**

7. **Please describe the company's original product/service line and any subsequent changes that have been made.**

   INVESTOR'S PERSPECTIVE
   Numerous changes in a company's product line can be either a positive or negative indication. Subtle changes to a functionally superior product line may reflect a strong product line supplemented by a well-thought out market ing plan. However, substantial ongoing changes may be symptomatic of serious problems. Management's loss of touch with the company's target market, declining demand, technical obsolescence, or superiority of competitors' products may be responsible for recurring changes. On the other hand, management sensitivity to rapid market evolution may justify frequent changes in the company's product line.

8. **Please provide the following information about each of the company's products/services: physical and functional description, distinctive characteristics that will serve to protect the company from a competitive contest with larger and**

better capitalized companies, susceptibility to obsolescence, cost effectiveness/overwhelming economic justification, patents issued and pending, proprietary content, brand/ trade names, standardization/compatibility, quality relative to the competition, estimated length and present phase of "life cycle," and convenience relative to the competition.

DEFINITIONS

Susceptibility to obsolescence—The vulnerability that a product or service has to a change in consumer behavior due to style, technology, price, or distribution.

Cost effectiveness/Overwhelming economic justification —The ability of a product or service to fulfill an essential need (e.g., not susceptible to a change in style or fashion) at less cost than the competition while offering equal or better quality than the competition.

Product life cycle—Recognition of the distinct phases in the sales history of a product or service. The four stages consist of introduction, growth, maturity, and decline. With each phase there are corresponding opportunities and problems with respect to marketing strategy and profit.

Typically, the company suffers losses through the introduction and early growth phases due to heavy start-up, organization, research, development, advertising, and promotion expenditures. During the latter growth stages, profits are achieved as existing purchasing patterns are changed and market penetration increases. Profits peak during maturity as competition, attracted by substantial profit margins, enters the market place. Finally, sales volume declines as the decrease in the volume of new buyers exceeds the number of replacement buyers, and newer products and services divert the interest of buyers from existing products.

Prices are usually highest during the introduction phase because of the lack of competition and the need for margins large enough to finance heavy promotional expenditures. During the growth phase profits increase due to proportionately lower promotional and production expense per unit, although absolute promotional expenditures will remain high. As competition increases during the maturity phase, prices decrease, and increased market segmentation replaces the emphasis on promotion. The decline stage is characterized by a reduction in competition and product selection. Profitability sometimes increases due to lower competition.

Because product life cycle is an abstract concept, it is best used as a forecasting and planning tool.

INVESTOR'S PERSPECTIVE

This is one of the most important factors that a prospective investor will consider. Investors prefer a quality product or service, at a reasonable price, that has demonstrable market need. Commercial, industrial products that directly reduce costs while maintaining or increasing quality are strong candidates for investment (e.g., computerized versus manual record keeping). The product should have a defensible market niche (e.g., it should be differentiated from the competition in some meaningful way[s]). Differences may include such things as quality, style, technology (patents), and price. Products/services with differences that are only perceived rather than real, or that are easy to duplicate, are thought to be highly risky by prospective investors.

9. **Please discuss the future potential of all promising new products/services that the company is now developing.**

INVESTOR'S PERSPECTIVE

An investor looks to future cash flow for return on investment. Future potential will depend on demand for the company's product, and management's ability to supply that product to the market at an economically justifiable price. Because most markets are characterized by continuous change, a company's ability to perceive new trends and develop, produce, and market new products, is extremely important.

10. **To what extent are the company, its officers, property, and products insured? Please list all policies that are presently in effect.**

INVESTOR'S PERSPECTIVE

Insurance, while reducing cash flow, does provide a limit on contingent downside liability.

11. **What are the advantages and disadvantages of the company's present locations (e.g., proximity to customers, suppli-**

ers, labor, energy sources, transportation; taxbreaks; special financial arrangements).

SOURCES
   Usually, the local Chamber of Commerce will provide most of the information requested above.

12. **What are the best sources to use for the purpose of researching the company's products/services and markets?**

INVESTOR'S PERSPECTIVE
   Below are some of the standard research sources available to business. The investor may want to know the specific research sources you consulted in the preparation of your business plan. It is essential to document as much as possible the information you use in your plan. Besides the sources listed below, other references could include books about your specific product and markets, summaries of proprietary market research, and reports from securities analysts about competitors in your field.

Standard & Poor's
25 Broadway
New York, NY
212/248-2525

Dun & Bradstreet
99 Church St
New York NY 10007
212/285-7000

Moody's Investor Service
99 Church Street
New York NY 10007
212/553-0300

The Insider's Guide to Small Business Resources,
Gumpert & Timmons,
Doubleday, 1982.

Business Reference Sources,
Harvard University,
Graduate School of
Business Administration,
   1971.

US Department of
  Commerce,
14th Street between
  Constitution Avenue and
  E Street N.W.
Washington, DC 20230
202/377-2000

US Small Business
  Administration
1441 L Street N.W.
Washington, DC 20416
202/653-6808

US Government Manual,
  1980–1981
Office of the Federal
  Register
National Archives and
  Records Service
General Services
  Administration
Washington, DC 20408

Finding Facts Fast,
Alden Todd,
Ten Speed Press, 1979.

Up the Organization,
Donald M. Dible,
California: The
  Entrepreneur Press,
1974, chapter 6, pages 63–
80.

Trade publications

Annual reports of publicly
  traded companies in the
  same Industry.

Business periodicals (e.g.,
  *Business Week, Fortune,
  Forbes, Wall Street
  Journal, Barron's*)

B. Legal
  1. Legal structure:
     proprietorship ☐ partnership ☐
     corporation ☐ other (please describe) ☐

       SOURCE
       For information on which structure best suits the company's situation, an attorney should be consulted.

  2. State(s) of incorporation:

  3. States in which the company is licensed to do business as a foreign corporation:

       Used in this context, the phrase *foreign corporation* means that a business is operating in a state other than the one where the business is incorporated.

  4. Describe fully all lawsuits and legal actions threatened or pending against the company, its directors, management, and principals.

       INVESTOR'S PERSPECTIVE
       Lawsuits seldom present anything but problems. As the plaintiff (entity seeking legal relief), a small business has to expend a great deal of time and money to protect its legal rights. For the defendant (entity against which legal relief is being sought for alleged wrongdoing), a lawsuit represents a contingent liability (potential loss).

  5. If any employees of the company are vulnerable to future lawsuits by former employers, please explain (e.g., violation of covenant not to compete, use of proprietary technology, divulgence of privileged information).

       DEFINITION
       Covenant not to compete—Many companies, especially high technology firms, suffer great losses when an employee leaves to join another company. The employee often takes with him existing customers, costly training, and vital secrets learned from his previous employer. An employee may be prevented from using or sharing such proprietary information if he/she previously signed a nondisclosure agreement. He/she can also be prevented, within certain limita-

tions, from using his/her expertise to form another competing firm if he/she previously signed a covenant not to compete. Such agreements and covenants are often executed before the employee is made privy to vital company secrets.

Thus, a start-up firm that hires away key employees from another company may be vulnerable to certain legal actions. Accordingly, an attorney should be consulted before potentially damaging actions are taken.

6. **Please explain all mergers, consolidations, and reorganizations that the company has gone through.**

INVESTOR'S PERSPECTIVE

Investors will look favorably on those companies whose mergers and acquisitions have contributed to profitability and growth. Explain in detail the conditions surrounding the merger or acquisition agreements, such as the cost of purchasing stock or any debt incurred during the process of merging with or acquiring a company.

7. **Please list all subsidiaries, divisions, and branches of the company, including names, addresses, dates established, products, functions, and percentages owned by the company.**

INVESTOR'S PERSPECTIVE

Listing all the subsidiaries and divisions of the firm provides an investor with an indication of how diversified the company is. A well-diversified firm can expect more stable earnings than a firm that relies on one product. For example, a firm that sells ice cream and hot chocolate can be expected to perform better than a firm that sells only ice cream. The reason? Both firms should do well in the summer, but only the more diversified firm—the one that sells hot chocolate in addition to ice cream—will do well in the winter. This example illustrates one of the dangers of seasonality—i.e., having a product or service that sells only during a particular time of year.

But seasonality is not the only example of how a firm may *not* be adequately diversified. Consider the case of a computer manufacturer that makes only dedicated word processors, i.e., computers devoted strictly to word processing. This company will meet stiff competition from computer manufacturers with a product that can perform other tasks besides word processing, such as financial calculations, data storage, and so on.

Thus if a firm has a diverse product base, it should emphasize how that diversity makes it a stronger company. If a firm has only one or two products, it should explain how those products are unique and how they can meet the challenge of a better diversified competitor. (See Chapter I, Question 8.)

8. Please describe, in detail, all franchise, royalty, license, and working agreements that are presently in effect.

INVESTOR'S PERSPECTIVE

As the licensee (user or distributor of another company's name, product, technology or business format in exchange for some form of compensation, e.g., royalty or license fee) a company acquires both additional assets and liabilities. The use of an established company's name and business format (e.g., McDonald's, Midas, H&R Block) can substantially add to the sales volume of a small business. However, in return, that small business is obligated to pay a royalty which is usually a fixed percentage of sales or unit volume regardless of the incremental profitability generated by the licensing agreement.

As the licensor (company that grants the use of its name, technology or process in exchange for compensation), a company can add to its revenue base without incurring additional fixed cost (e.g., add to its own capacity by acquiring plant and equipment). However, licensing a company that does not maintain the same level of quality control could seriously damage the licensor's image.

9. Please discuss the assignability of the company's beneficial agreements (e.g., licenses, royalty agreements, franchise agreements, employment contracts, suppliers' contracts, leases, etc.).

DEFINITION

Assignability—Permission from one party to transfer its rights with a second party to a third party. For example, a franchisor may not permit a franchisee to sell its rights as a franchisee to a third party.

INVESTOR'S PERSPECTIVE

If a company can sell, or assign for collateral purposes, its license to use a valuable name, technology, or process, it will own an asset that increases both its market value and borrowing power. This hidden value is seldom reflected on the company's balance sheet.

II. MANAGEMENT

A. For each officer of the company, please provide the following information: name, age, number of years' direct experience in the company's industry, number of years with company, terms of employment contract with company, responsibilities/functions of position held with company, loans or advances to company, ownership interest in company (i.e., number of shares, warrants, stock options, etc.); salary, bonus, pension benefits, profit sharing, life insurance, stock bonuses, and perquisites to be received from company; unique qualities, abilities, experience and education that will be contributed to the management team. Include a diagram, where applicable, reflecting the organization of the company's management team by name, title, and function and other supporting documentation as an exhibit in appendix I.

> *INVESTOR'S PERSPECTIVE*
> The quality of management is probably the single most important factor that an investor will consider. To most investors, "class A management with a class B product is preferable to class B management with a class A product." Typically the team should be divided along the lines of the firm: marketing, finance, and operations. The ultimate success of any product or venture will depend on the abilities and commitment of the management team. Naturally, an investor looks for an experienced management team with a proven track record.

13

The investor also prefers upper management with a substantial ownership position. This will act as both compensation tied to performance and an incentive for key personnel to stay with the company.

B. What are the ultimate personal objectives of each officer, shareholder, and director, relative to the company (e.g., go public in five years, buy out other investors, build an industry-leading company, sell out to a larger competitor, make state-of-the-art technology available to the public)?

INVESTOR'S PERSPECTIVE

Investors prefer management with objectives similar to their own—for example, maximizing return on investment by positioning the company to go public in five years rather than concentrating on new technologies that do not necessarily have commercial applications.

C. Please provide the following information about each director who is *not* also an officer of the company: name, age, corporate affiliation, compensation by company, ownership interest in company (e.g., number of shares, warrants, stock options), special contributions to management.

INVESTOR'S PERSPECTIVE

Investors prefer to see a board of directors that can add expertise, experience, and personal connections to the management resources of the company.

D. What are the strengths and weaknesses of both the company's management team and its board of directors?

INVESTOR'S PERSPECTIVE

Investors prefer a management team that can both identify and compensate for its shortcomings. An entrepreneur should not ignore or hide the weaknesses of the firm's management.

E. Please describe all significant changes in the management of the company that have occurred over the last five years.

INVESTOR'S PERSPECTIVE
Repeated changes in the management team are viewed as an indication of instability. Occasional additions to the core management team may be viewed as an improvement depending on the capabilities of new personnel and associated levels of compensation.

F. References will be contacted for the purpose of obtaining additional information about the company, its products/services, and the integrity/capability of management. For each member of the company's management team, list as many individual references as possible in the following categories: accountants, lawyers, bankers, other lenders, former employers, former employees, former business partners, trade association personnel, venture capitalists, consultants, customers, competitors, and suppliers. Please provide names of individual contacts, firm names, addresses, phone numbers, and an explanation of the basis for each relationship (e.g., social acquaintance, business acquaintance, fellow club/organization member). Include letters of recommendation and other supporting documentation as an exhibit in appendix I.**

INVESTOR'S PERSPECTIVE
A diverse group of well-respected professional references is preferable to a list of social acquaintances.

G. Please list the organizations that will be providing professional counsel to the company (e.g., legal, accounting, advertising, public relations, banking, insurance).

INVESTOR'S PERSPECTIVE
Quality professional help, although possibly more expensive, will increase the company's probability of success. In addition to direct benefits, professionals also offer introductions to potentially helpful individuals and organizations (e.g., customers, suppliers, and distributors).

H. How will the company build a larger and more proficient management team during the next five to seven years?

INVESTOR'S PERSPECTIVE
    In addition to growing beyond their capital bases, most small businesses fail because they outgrow the capabilities of their management team. Therefore the successes of rapidly growing businesses will be confined to their ability to attract and train new management.

I. **Please discuss conflicts of interest that members of the company's management team or board of directors may have (e.g., other business interests, related party transactions, etc.).**

DEFINITION
    Conflicts of interest—Conflicts of interest exist when an individual owes his/her loyalties to more than one firm. When such conflicts exist, the fiduciary relationship between the employer and the employee is endangered. One example of a conflict of interest would occur when an employee of one firm buys goods from a second firm, of which he/she is a member of the board of directors. Thus, his/her ability to conduct business in an unbiased manner is open to question. Such practices are vulnerable to legal action by shareholders and creditors, as well as government agencies.
    Fiduciary—A person having a duty, created by his/her undertaking, to act primarily for the benefit of another.

J. **If any member of the management team will not be devoting 100% of his time to the company, please explain why.**

INVESTOR'S PERSPECTIVE
    Investors usually demand that management devote 110% of its efforts to the company.

K. **How will the company protect itself from the prospect of future competition with defecting members of its management team (e.g., covenant not to compete, nondisclosure agreement)?**

INVESTOR'S PERSPECTIVE
    Many successful firms face competition from firms created by their former employees. Lack of protection is a liability.

III. OWNERSHIP

INVESTOR'S PERSPECTIVE

Smaller businesses, start-up companies, and companies going through periods of rapid growth are viewed as risk-intensive. Universally, investors expect the assumption of higher risk to offer the opportunity for greater return. Accordingly, investors usually seek current yield (e.g., interest on debt) and/or equity appreciation (e.g., ownership of a portion of the company in anticipation of an increase in the value of the company). There are a variety of debt/equity instruments that can be used to accommodate both the company seeking capital and the investor. The company's principals should familiarize themselves with the basic instruments and their particular characteristics to facilitate the negotiation process.

SOURCES

Most beginning and intermediate accounting and finance books provide detailed explanations of the various debt/equity instruments.

A. Please list all current and prospective owners (including individuals, corporations, trusts, etc.) of the company's common and preferred stock, and the number of shares owned or available

under warrants conversion privileges and employee stock bonus/option agreements.

DEFINITIONS

Common Stock—Ownership rights in the company issued to investors in return for capital. As the owners, shareholders have the right to elect the company's board of directors, who in turn appoint top management. Thus, the entrepreneur is in effect trading away a specified degree of control over the management of the company in exchange for the capital necessary to make the firm grow.

Common stockholders have residual rights to the net income and net assets of the company subject to restrictions imposed by the contractual rights of creditors, employees, and other interested parties. The stockholders' return is not fixed in amount or specified as to date. However, if the company is liquidated, creditors' claims, and the claims of preferred stockholders, usually have priority. Conversely, no matter how successful the company, a creditor's return will be limited to principal and interest. Thus, the common stockholder assumes greater risk than a creditor, but has an opportunity for greater return. Common stock is the most risk-intensive investment vehicle, but it also has the potential for the largest reward.

Preferred Stock—Similar to common stock, preferred shares are issued by the company in exchange for capital. Although the characteristics of preferred stock may vary widely, preferred shareholders rarely participate in the election of the company's board of directors. Usually preferred shareholders are entitled to a fixed dividend (similar to interest on debt) and/or proceeds from the liquidation of the company's assets (up to a specified maximum per share) after creditors receive payment but before common stockholders receive their share of the liquidation proceeds (if any proceeds are available after satisfying creditors and preferred shareholders). The dividend "preference" is usually cumulative, meaning all back dividends must be paid to the preferred shareholders before common shareholders receive dividend distributions. Unlike debt, preferred stock does not entitle the holder to insist on dividend or "principal" payment by specified dates. Some preferred stocks have conversion privileges, which allow shareholders to convert preferred shares into common shares by use of a specified formula (e.g., two shares of preferred for one share of common). Certain debt instruments carry similar conversion privileges (e.g., $100 of principal for one share of common). Conversion privileges are used to increase the appeal of standard debt and preferred stock instruments to investors.

Employee Stock Bonuses—Generally used as an additional form of employee compensation, stock bonuses consist of shares of common stock that are given to employees as a reward for outstanding performance. Stock bonuses offer rapidly growing companies a variety of benefits. In addition to direct benefits as a performance incentive, stock ownership rewards employees for the overall success of the company through appreciation of share value. Stock ownership also provides employees with an additional incentive to remain with the company. For small, rapidly growing companies, stock bonuses prove an opportunity to compensate employee performance without depleting scarce cash flow.

Employee Stock Options—Similar to stock bonuses, stock options are used as an additional form of employee compensation. An option entitles the holder to purchase a specified amount of common stock, at a specified price, by a specified date. The holder hopes that appreciation of the market price of the underlying common stock will increase beyond the specified option price, resulting in substantial profits for the employee. Benefits to the company are also similar to those of a stock bonus plan.

Warrants—Similar to stock options, warrants entitle the holder to purchase a specified number of common shares, at a specified price, by a specified date. However, warrants are usually offered to investors in combination with other instruments as an additional incentive. In this case warrants offer greater return without increased investment. Thus, a company that offers its common stock to investors may increase the number of shares sold by including one warrant for every five common shares purchased.

INVESTOR'S PERSPECTIVE

Investors considering purchase of the company's stock will want to compute its ownership position as a percentage of present and future ("fully diluted") shares outstanding. This figure, when used in conjunction with financial projections, will allow the investor to calculate expected return on investment.

B. Please describe all significant changes in the ownership of the company that have occurred over the last five years.

INVESTOR'S PERSPECTIVE
Frequent ownership changes are an indication of instability.

C. Please explain what protection investors have against future dilution of their ownership position (e.g., preemptive rights).

DEFINITION
Dilution—If an investor owns 10 shares out of a total 100 outstanding, he/she owns 10% of the company (10/100 = 10%). If the company subsequently sells another hundred shares to a third party, the investor's position will be reduced ("diluted") to 5% (10/200 = 5%).
Preemptive Rights—An existing stockholder is given the right of first refusal on subsequent stock offerings in proportion to his/her ownership percentage prior to the offering. For example, in the above illustration, the investor would be offered 10 of 100 shares sold to maintain its 10% ownership position.

D. Please discuss any restriction on the transferability or collateral value of the company's shares.

DEFINITION
Restriction on Transferability—Certain securities laws restrict the sale or transfer of stock, especially stock not registered with the SEC. Since the stock of most small businesses is not registered, the market is severely limited.

E. Please discuss any buy/sell agreements that pertain to the company's shares.

INVESTOR'S PERSPECTIVE
Properly structured, a buy/sell agreement provides for the future sale of a business upon the death or departure of one of the principals. Often financed through a life insurance plan covering the principals, the agreement provides for an orderly transfer of business interests to a designated heir, employee, stockholder, or partner. These agreements enhance the value of the firm to investors because they assure continuity of the firm's ownership.

F. Do the company's shares have cumulative voting rights?

DEFINITION
Cumulative Voting Rights—Under cumulative voting, simultaneous elections are held for all board positions, and each share of stock represents as many votes as there are board positions. Votes can be accumulated by minority shareholders and cast in favor of one particular candidate, thus insuring the election of at least one board member who will represent the minority shareholders.

$$(5 \text{ board positions}) \times (1000 \text{ shares}) = 5000 \text{ votes}$$

In the election of any one board member position, a 51% majority can be obtained with only 505 votes, thus insuring the election of a particular candidate. A 505-vote majority can be accumulated with only 505/5 or 101 shares. Thus a 10% minority contingent of shares can obtain representation on the board under cumulative voting.

If a firm does not have cumulative voting rights, each share of stock represents one vote for purposes of electing the board of directors. Separate elections are held for each board position, making it very difficult for minority shareholders to obtain representation on the board.

G. Please explain the company's employee stock ownership plan.

DEFINITION
An *Employee Stock Ownership Plan* (ESOP) and/or an *Employee Stock Ownership Trust* (ESOT) are vehicles that a

company can use to shift ownership from a small control group to the company's employees. In addition to some very favorable tax benefits, ESOPs and ESOTs represent another method of raising equity capital while simultaneously providing ownership incentives to employees. An attorney should be consulted for discussion of the many complexities involved.

IV. EMPLOYEES

INVESTOR'S PERSPECTIVE

Investors prefer a highly elastic labor force, one that can be readily increased or decreased depending on the firm's economic cycle. Because they limit flexibility, union affiliations are usually perceived as a liability from the investor's point of view. Hence, an abundance of both skilled and unskilled labor in the local labor market, in combination with a minimum training requirement for the company's work force, would present a highly flexible situation that could be adjusted to the company's needs on short notice. In any case, the company's employees are an invaluable resource that should be fully utilized through progressive recruiting, training, evaluation, and compensation programs.

A. **How many individuals have been/will be employed by the company over the last three years (actual) and the next three years (projected)?**

	Actual		
Date of Fiscal Year End	_____	_____	_____
Full-time Employees	_____	_____	_____
Part-time Employees	_____	_____	_____

	Projected		
Date of Fiscal Year End	_____	_____	_____
Full-time Employees	_____	_____	_____
Part-time Employees	_____	_____	_____

B. **What percent of total employees will be skilled vs unskilled over the next three years?**

Date of Fiscal Year End	_____	_____	_____
Skilled Employees	_____	_____	_____
Unskilled Employees	_____	_____	_____

INVESTOR'S PERSPECTIVE
Skilled employees may be more difficult to locate and train and may also demand higher salaries. Unskilled labor is usually perceived as less reliable and more transient. Accordingly, management is less likely to lay off or terminate skilled than unskilled labor during economic downturns.

C. **What are the company's union affiliations?**

D. **What has been/will be the company's direct labor cost as a percent of sales during both the last three years (actual) and the next three years (projected)?**

Actual

Date of Fiscal Year End	_____	_____	_____
Direct Labor as a Percent of Sales	_____	_____	_____

Projected

Date of Fiscal Year End	_____	_____	_____
Direct Labor as a Percent of Sales	_____	_____	_____

INVESTOR'S PERSPECTIVE

If most of the company's cost of goods/services sold is attributable to labor costs, it is "labor-intensive." If most of the company's cost of goods/services sold is attributable to investment in machinery, plant and equipment, it is "capital-intensive." Labor intensity may indicate an opportunity for increased productivity through automation.

Also, a labor-intensive operation is sometimes thought to be more flexible during economic contractions because employees can be laid off or terminated more easily than machinery, plant, and equipment can be sold and later repurchased. Others argue that certain employee benefits, union agreements, and pension fund liabilities make both options equally unattractive.

E. **Please describe the local labor market and how it affects the company (e.g., cost of labor relative to other parts of the country, skilled and unskilled labor availability, and union concentration).**

F. **Please describe all benefits/perquisites that are made available to employees (e.g., pension plan, profit-sharing plan, employee stock ownership plan, life/medical insurance, subsidized lunches, on-premises employee athletic facilities).**

G. **How does the company's compensation program compare with the market (i.e., salary plus benefits/perquisites)?**

INVESTOR'S PERSPECTIVE
Larger companies claim that employee benefits account for up to one-third of their employee compensation package. Accordingly, smaller companies that do not provide comparable salary levels *and comparable benefits* may have great difficulty in attracting qualified employees.

H. If the company requires any highly skilled employees, please discuss their functions, anticipated compensation, and the degree of difficulty involved in both locating and hiring qualified personnel.

INVESTOR'S PERSPECTIVE
The greater the scarcity and compensation of certain key employees, the more vulnerable the company will be to crippling personnel losses. If a company relies heavily on highly skilled personnel, an investor will want to know how the company's management plans to retain and attract such key employees. For example, an entrepreneur may show an investor that his company's wages and benefits for key employees are better than those of the industry as a whole. He may also demonstrate to an investor that his company's geographical location attracts a substantial pool of skilled workers.

I. Please provide the history and current status of the company's labor relations, including any strikes or work stoppages.

INVESTOR'S PERSPECTIVE
A history of strikes and work stoppages suggests that there are problems within the firm that management has failed to rectify. In any case, investors will be wary of recurring labor problems that could reduce productivity, cause work stoppages, and damage employee morale.

J. How easily can the size of the company's labor force be adjusted to fluctuations in sales volume?

INVESTOR'S PERSPECTIVE
   Investors perceive management's ability to conserve the company's scarce cash flow during economic downturns by reducing the labor force as a substantial asset.

K. Please discuss the company's historical labor turnover.

INVESTOR'S PERSPECTIVE
   Frequent labor turnover can detract from productivity and employee morale. Costs required to train replacement employees can be substantial.

L. Please describe the company's employee training and development program.

INVESTOR'S PERSPECTIVE
   Training and development programs should include objective, quantifiable methods of measuring progress coupled with commensurate rewards. Employees should feel that they are both fairly judged and fairly rewarded.

V. INVESTMENT CRITERIA

INVESTOR'S PERSPECTIVE
 If the best of business opportunities is not properly structured, it will attract little attention from investors. Accordingly, the company's principals should have an idea of how prospective investors prefer to structure their deals. Although final terms are subject to negotiation, the company's principals should determine what they are willing to give up on what terms before meeting with prospective investors.
 Claims on the firm's financial rewards will be sought in return for the investor's capital. Such claims can take the form of either equity or debt. If it is equity, as is the case with most venture capital firms, then an investor looks to increased future earnings. If it is debt, as is the case with banks, then an investor looks to collateral and cash flow to cover principal and interest payments. Equity holders seek appreciation while debt holders seek interest and repayment of principal.

A. General
 1. On a fully diluted basis, approximately what percent of the company is the present ownership group offering to its investors?

DEFINITION

Fully Diluted—Assumes that all warrants, options, conversion rights and bonus plans are exercised. Thus, in the earnings-per-share calculations, the number of shares is the sum of the number of shares actually outstanding plus shares potentially outstanding.

2. **How many shares of the company's common stock will remain authorized but not issued after this offering?**

DEFINITION

The number of shares authorized by the board of directors determines the maximum number that may be issued. The company is not obligated to issue the full number of shares authorized.

3. **What collateral (include approximate current market values) and letters of credit/personal guarantees are principals/investors willing to offer?**

INVESTOR'S PERSPECTIVE

When loaning money to the company in return for repayment of principal plus interest, investors who use debt instruments look to cash flow as their primary source of repayment, and collateral as their secondary source of repayment. These investors look favorably on personal guarantees; they view such guarantees as a performance bond that makes the principals think twice before walking away from the company during difficult times. On the other hand, equity investors—those who seek return in the form of appreciation of the company's stock—are not as likely to rely on the availability of collateral.

4. **Please discuss the purpose(s) for which proceeds will be used (e.g., general working capital needs, marketing, research and development, capital equipment).**

INVESTOR'S PERSPECTIVE

How the company spends investors' funds directly affects the level of risk associated with that investment. For example, an expenditure of funds on research and development or advertising would not produce the marketable asset value of an expenditure on real estate and machinery. Therefore, investments that will be used to pay for "intangibles" are thought to be riskier than those used to purchase "hard assets."

5. **Please list all capital sources (e.g., banks, finance companies, individuals, venture capital companies, the selling group) that have either committed or disbursed funds to the company in the form of debt/equity, and the amounts (original/ current) and terms of their commitments (e.g., pricing, collateral, amortization schedule, restrictive covenants, percentage of total equity purchased, conversion features, call provisions).**

DEFINITIONS

Amortization Schedule—A schedule used to calculate the amounts and dates of interest and principal payments that must be made to retire a loan over a specified time period. This schedule represents a contractual agreement between the lender and the borrower. Accordingly, the borrower's failure to make a scheduled payment constitutes default and entitles the lender to pursue its legal remedies.

Restrictive Covenants—Restrictions on the borrower that are in force during the life of the loan agreement. These restrictions may prevent the firm from issuing additional debt, selling its fixed assets, paying dividends to shareholders, or engaging in any activity that reduces the firm's ability to repay its loan.

Call Provisions—Similar to a standard bond, a "callable" bond legally obligates the borrowing company to a specified amortization schedule. However, a "call provision" entitles the company to repay principal before the scheduled maturity date. Naturally, the company would only retire a "callable" bond that could be refinanced more cheaply (e.g., if market interest rates fall or if the market price for the company's stock increases). Any gains received by the company through the "call provision" will be at the expense of the investor who must reinvest his principal at lower market interest rates. Thus, investors find "callable bonds" to be less attractive and would expect a "callable" bond to carry a higher interest rate than a standard bond.

Conversion Features—Investors sometimes prefer to purchase investment instruments (e.g., convertible debentures, convertible preferred stock) that provide for return through different sources (e.g., interest, appreciation in value of common stock). These instruments can usually be converted from one form of return to another, at the investor's option. Please see Section III A under "definition of preferred stock" for additional information.

6. **Please provide a list of all companies/individuals from which the company has sought but not received financing and associated explanations of why the company's requests were rejected.**

    INVESTOR'S PERSPECTIVE
    Companies that have "shopped the market" for investors with little success are viewed negatively by prospective investors. Therefore, the company must be extremely well prepared for its initial investor meetings rather than learning about the investment industry as it moves from prospective investor to prospective investor.

B. Terms

1. **Total amount of financing requested from all sources for the next three years.**

2. **Preferred form of requested financing:**

	Dollar Amount	Percent of Total Financing
Debt	_____	_____
Equity	_____	_____
Convertible Debt	_____	_____

3. Date(s) needed by (if multiple takedowns are feasible, list schedule of dates, amounts, and purposes):

INVESTOR'S PERSPECTIVE

Investors usually prefer to "stage" cash infusions rather than disbursing funds in a lump sum. This practice allows the investor to withhold future disbursements if the company does not live up to expectations.

Amount	Date	Purpose
_____	_____	_____
_____	_____	_____
_____	_____	_____
_____	_____	_____
_____	_____	_____
_____	_____	_____
_____	_____	_____

VI. MARKET AND COMPETITION

1. Is the company dominant in its field?

DEFINITION

Market Share—Represents the percentage of the total market that the company serves on a dollar sales basis or on a unit sales basis. A firm is said to be dominant if it controls the largest market share. The difficulty lies in defining exactly what market the company serves. A hot dog stand and a hamburger stand may both serve the fast food market, yet they also serve autonomous hot dog and hamburger markets. The firms might be dominant in each of their respective markets while only one firm is dominant in the fast food market.

Several studies have demonstrated the link between dominant market share and increased profitability. IBM achieves greater profitability through its economies of scale in production and advertising by spreading the costs of these functions across a larger number of units sold. By devoting its greater resources to research and development, IBM is also able to set the industry standard for innovative technology and quality. Thus, it can demand a premium for its products in the market place that will further perpetuate its dominance over the industry.

"Market share" strategies for new products vary. Management may elect to keep prices relatively low while building market share to prevent competitors from entering the market. After establishing a dominant market share, the company can afford to compete on superior terms and therefore justify a price increase. However, others believe that while a company with a new product has the entire market to itself, it should charge a premium price to recapture its development costs as quickly as possible. This strategy may be appropriate if the company has proprietary protection or another significant competitive edge.

2. **Please provide management's estimate of the company's market share and associated industry rank for both the last three years (actual) and the next three years (projected).**

Actual

Date of Fiscal
Year End   _____ _____ _____

Market Share   _____ _____ _____

Industry Rank   _____ _____ _____

Projected

Date of Fiscal
Year End   _____ _____ _____

Market Share   _____ _____ _____

Industry Rank   _____ _____ _____

B. **Competition**

1. **Please list the following information about the company's five major competitors: ownership, approximate annual volume, market share, and profitability.**

DEFINITION
As explained above, the market and relevant competition can be defined in a variety of different ways. Definitions should be adjusted to the availability of reliable data.

INVESTOR'S PERSPECTIVE
Entry into an industry characterized by well-capitalized, established competitors is viewed as risk intensive. Investors prefer companies that are entering into new, poorly organized industries in which established leaders have not yet emerged.

a. _____

Name   **Estimated Annual Volume**

_____

Address

_____

City, State

_____

Net Profit as a Percentage of Sales   **Market Share**

b. _____

Name   **Estimated Annual Volume**

_____

Address

_____

City, State

_____

Net Profit as a Percentage of Sales   **Market Share**

c. _____

Name   **Estimated Annual Volume**

_____

Address

_____

City, State

_____

Net Profit as a Percentage of Sales   **Market Share**

d. _____

Name   **Estimated Annual**
                                                            Volume

_____

Address

_____

City, State

_____

Net Profit as a Percentage of Sales   **Market Share**

e. _____

Name   **Estimated Annual**
                                                            Volume

_____

Address

_____

City, State

_____

Net Profit as a Percentage of Sales   **Market Share**

2. **In tabular form, please compare the company's strengths and weaknesses with those of its major competitors (e.g., products/services, quality and depth of management, financial resources, production economies, advertising/promotion program, market penetration, sales/distribution network, and research and development commitment).**

DEFINITION

Production Economies—The ability of a company to produce greater volume at a decreasing cost per unit. The cost incurred by firms in the production of its products/services consists of both a fixed and a variable component. As volume increases, variable costs also rise but fixed costs remain relatively constant. Hence, the total cost per unit decreases. A company that achieves production economies can respond to market competition by producing more goods at a lower cost, thus capturing an increased market share. If other firms fail to respond competitively by lowering their prices or differentiating the value component of their particular brand, the high-volume firm will be able to build and maintain a dominant unit market share while simultaneously increasing profitability.

Market Penetration—Determines how much market share a company controls. Greater penetration of a market can be achieved by:

1 Attracting new customers to the industry
2 Attracting existing customers from competitors
3 Increasing the volume of purchases by existing customers

Each of these objectives requires a somewhat different marketing mix. To entirely new customers, the product attributes being stressed must appeal to the general need to be satisfied, e.g., "personal computers will increase productivity." To existing personal computer users, the marketing mix must center around the advantages of a particular brand, e.g., "Apple computers have the best software." And, to existing Apple customers, the advertising message should strive to maintain their loyalty while increasing the purchase of Apple accessories and updated versions of previously purchased models.

Sales/Distribution Networks—Networks link a producer of goods to its buyers and provide the means through which an organization implements its marketing strategy. A network should provide the best coverage of target markets at a reasonable cost. Firms may use direct mail, intermediaries, or their own captive sales force to reach buyers. Intermediaries consist of brokers, dealers, distributors, and wholesalers. Intermediaries are usually less expensive than a captive sales force because training costs are far lower, compensation is basically tied to commissions, and costs are usually spread among other noncompetitive lines. Thus, intermediaries are an appropriate choice for a start-up firm or for a firm selling nontechnical products. However, for technical products requiring sophisticated training, the best choice is probably a captive sales force trained directly by the manufacturer.

INVESTOR'S PERSPECTIVE

By comparing the company's strengths and weaknesses with those of its competitors, the investor can better determine the company's probability of success as well as the attainability of its strategic plan. Also, recognition of the company's own weaknesses reflects on management's honesty and capability.

3. **Relative to the competition, what margins will be realized on the company's products/services by retailers and wholesalers, and how will the company compensate salesmen, manufacturers' representatives/distributors (e.g., base salary, commission, car, club membership, etc.)? Accordingly, what responsibilities will the above personnel assume (e.g., warranty service, accounts receivable, collection, inventory financing, warehousing.)?**

DEFINITION

Margin—The difference between revenues received and expenses incurred. *Gross margin* is the difference between total sales revenue and the total cost of goods sold. It may be expressed as a dollar amount or as a percentage. *Net margin* is the difference between sales revenues and virtually all costs related to the production of those revenues such as materials, labor, utilities, interest, administration, and taxes. As with the gross margin, it may be expressed as a percentage or as a total dollar amount.

INVESTOR'S PERSPECTIVE

Without effective distribution, the best product or service will not reach its full growth potential. Accordingly, if salesmen are not adequately compensated, they will be motivated to sell competing lines that offer higher margins. However, to minimize fixed expenses, the company should tie compensation of its salesmen and distributors to performance (e.g., small base salary with large commissions). Smaller businesses may also want to offer larger profit margins to distributors in exchange for other expense-reducing services (e.g., warranty service and accounts receivable collection by the distributor in exchange for price concessions from the manufacturer). It should be noted that industry practice often dictates the method and amount of salesmen/distributor compensation.

C. Market definition

1. **What was/will be the approximate size, in units and dollars, of the total market for each of the company's products/**

services for both the last three years (actual) and the next three years (projected)? Include market surveys, test market results, feasibility studies, trade association reports, government market data, and other supporting documentation as an exhibit in appendix I.

DEFINITION

Total Market—A market consists of prospective buyers who are willing and able to purchase a company's goods/services. The definition centers around buyers, not products. Thus, if the buyers' needs shift and the organization finds demand for its products slipping, the organization must develop a new product line that better meets the needs of its market. Thus, the firm must always define its market and center its marketing plans around buyers and their anticipated needs.

INVESTOR'S PERSPECTIVE

Investors prefer a broad market with both a previous history and future expectations of growth exceeding 20% per year. Smaller market growth rates are acceptable if the company is clearly a leader in its industry with a history of increasing market share. The investor will evaluate the market on the basis of several criteria in addition to the size and growth of the market: strength of the competition, number of competitors, profit margins, obstacles to entry (e.g., technical, proprietary, financial). The investor will then decide whether the company's strengths, weaknesses, and overall strategic plan are complementary with its market. For example, the consumer products industry is dominated by marketing giants such as Proctor & Gamble, Colgate, and Lever Brothers. Unless a competitor can afford to match multimillion dollar advertising budgets, it should consider another industry.

SOURCES

US Department of Commerce
14th Street Between Constitution
   Avenue & E Street N.W.
Washington, DC 20230
202/377-2000

Trade publications

Major business periodicals

2. **In what geographic areas are the company's sales concentrated?**

   INVESTOR'S PERSPECTIVE

   The size and nature of a market's geography are important considerations that must be factored into the company's marketing plan. For instance, the appropriate marketing mix will differ considerably when marketing a product to rural versus urban areas, or the East Coast versus the Deep South. When introducing a new product nationally, great care must be taken to introduce the product gradually to selected regions of the country where the company's distribution is the strongest, and where advertising dollars can be most effectively spent.

   Investors almost always view concentration as a liability and diversification as an asset. Concentration increases a company's vulnerability to economic downturns in a specialized sector of the economy. For example, if a company markets its products exclusively in the midwest, high unemployment in the basic manufacturing industries would have a more severe impact on the company than if it also marketed its products in the "high tech" areas of the sun belt.

3. **What has been the growth and profitability history of the company's major markets, and what are its future prospects? If the projected growth rate exceeds the historical growth rate, discuss the major factors behind the company's assumptions (e.g., technological breakthroughs, economic developments).**

   DEFINITION

   Technological Breakthrough—A technological innovation that enables a company to produce its goods/services at lower cost and/or in less time while maintaining or increasing quality. The hand-held calculator market experienced many technological breakthroughs that led to mass production techniques and resultant lower prices to the consumer. Breakthroughs enable newer firms to compete on a more efficient basis than established rivals, thereby offsetting the greater financial resources and broader marketing base of established competitors.

   INVESTOR'S PERSPECTIVE

   Investors look for companies that service rapidly growing markets.

4. **Please rank, in the order of importance, reasons why customers have purchased/will purchase the company's products/ services (e.g., quality, service, price, styling).**

    INVESTOR'S PERSPECTIVE
    To serve its market best, the company must constantly update its understanding of why customers purchase its products/services. Companies that lose touch with their customers expose themselves to loss of market share via increased market penetration by competitors.

5. **What underlying market needs are satisfied by the company's products/services?**

    INVESTOR'S PERSPECTIVE
    Products/services are often purchased for other than functional reasons. Charles Revson, former president of Revlon, once stated: "In the factory we make cosmetics, and in the drug store we sell hope." Expensive cars sometimes sell for the status they represent rather than their superior engineering. Rugged outdoor wear is occasionally purchased for the macho image it projects rather than its durability. Certainly, if the company is aware of the underlying needs that affect customers' purchasing habits, it can more effectively market its products/services.

6. **What are the social, behavioral, and demographic characteristics of the company's customer base/target market?**

    DEFINITION
    Market Characteristics—Markets may be divided into sectors referred to as market segments. Each segment is considered to possess a homogeneous characteristic affecting purchasing behavior. Marketing strategies can be developed to focus on the needs and characteristics of a particular market segment. Markets may be segmented according to geographic area (north versus south), demographic characteristics (older versus younger, male versus female, single versus married), behavioral characteristics (introvert versus extrovert), socioeconomic classification (high income versus low income). Markets can also be segmented according to consumer groups that perceive the product as offering differing attributes (e.g., status versus economy transportation). The key question in effective segmentation is, "Can the company's products be more effec-

tively marketed by developing different marketing strategies for each segment, or is it less expensive and more
efficient to develop a more general strategy?"

INVESTOR'S PERSPECTIVE
Management's ability to define accurately and to segment its market is essential to the company's sustained
growth and market penetration. A complete answer to this
question will help an investor evaluate the quality of the
company's marketing strategy.

**7. How will the company's management both monitor and ad-
just to significant changes in its customer base?**

INVESTOR'S PERSPECTIVE
Markets are dynamic rather than static. A company
that does not monitor and adjust to changes in its customer
base will suffer shrinking rather than increasing market
share.

**8. What significant changes are anticipated by management in
the company's customer base over the next five to seven
years?**

INVESTOR'S PERSPECTIVE
Management should have a familiarity with future
trends before they fully develop. The earlier preparation
can begin, the more effective it will be.

D. Market strategy

**1. Relative to the competition, how will the company's
products/services be marketed (i.e., comparative pricing,
promotional methods, trade show participation, advertising
effort, distribution channels/sales organization, private label
arrangements, standard sales terms, discounts offered, advertising allowance policy, customer service/warranty program,
return privileges, consignment sales)?**

DEFINITIONS
Comparative Pricing—How the company's prices com-
pare with those of its competitors.
Promotional Methods—Everything from free publicity

in local media to a nationally orchestrated coupon program.

Trade Show Participation—Sometimes provides effective forum for introduction of the company's products to distributors, wholesalers, retailers, and end users.

Private Label Arrangements—Rather than incurring substantial marketing expense, a manufacturer will sometimes agree to sell its product under a retailer's name. For example, many manufacturers sell their products under the Sears name.

Standard Sales Terms—Example: 2/10 net 30. Translates to a 2% discount off the face amount of an invoice if paid within 10 days of issuance. If not discounted within ten days, the full balance is due and payable within 30 days. Discount offers for prompt payment should reflect short-term interest rates.

Advertising Allowance Policy—Manufacturers sometimes offer distributors and retailers a rebate, against product purchased, for the purpose of advertising the company's product. For example, a manufacturer may offer a 2% rebate on all orders over $100,000 to be used for advertising within 90 days of the purchase.

Customer Service/Warranty Program—Although essential in many cases, especially for a technical product, a comprehensive service/warranty program can represent a significant contingent liability. If a company's products are inferior, service required under warranty and product returns may cause severe financial damage.

Return Privileges/Consignment Sales—Consignment sales provide for return by retailers of unsold merchandise. Besides creating a large contingent liability, this arrangement severely distorts interim financial profit and loss data.

INVESTOR'S PERSPECTIVE

Investors prefer to invest in a company that has thoroughly evaluated all the methods available to sell its products. Make sure to explain clearly why a specific method of marketing a product is essential. For example, if a company manufactures building insulation, it will want to display its product at various trade shows. If a company makes video display terminals, it will need to offer customer service and warranty programs to keep pace with the competition.

2. **How will the company's products/services be positioned in the marketplace relative to the competition over the next five to seven years? What will be their unique selling propositions as compared to similar products/services offered by the competition?**

   DEFINITIONS
   Product Positioning—Identifying and emphasizing various attributes of a product for the purpose of establishing a brand image. For example, nine out of ten colas may emphasize taste attributes while one cola emphasizes its low caffeine content. The low-caffeine product has positioned itself as the "healthier" alternative. Positioning sometimes permits virtually identical products to distinguish themselves through effective marketing.

   Unique Selling Proposition—In order to establish a brand image, a company may develop a unique selling proposition based on particular attributes of the product.

   INVESTOR'S PERSPECTIVE
   An effectively positioned product can achieve a dominant market share even in an industry characterized by similar products. Although product distinctions may be perceived rather than real, positioning can be used to create defensible niches in the absence of proprietary or technical support.

3. **Provide an analysis of how the company's management plans to capitalize on competitors' weaknesses and how it will meet the challenges represented by competitors' strengths.**

   INVESTOR'S PERSPECTIVE
   This issue seems self-evident, but many business plans fail to explain adequately the strengths and weakenesses of the competition. Investors are especially wary of business plans that do not discuss the strengths of the compeition— such an omission may appear to an investor as evidence of a "pie in the sky" attitude on the part of the company's management.

4. **Please discuss reasonably foreseeable competitive breakthroughs and how the company's management will protect the market share of its product/services from the continued development and improvement of competitive products/services.**

INVESTOR'S PERSPECTIVE

Competitive breakthroughs may pose a threat to the firm's position in the market and ultimately the firm's survival. Therefore, the company should create both a formal method of monitoring its market for breakthroughs and an internal research and development program. Breakthroughs may also serve to bring more consumers into the market, thereby increasing the customer base.

5. **What negative customer reactions have been received/are anticipated by the company's management, and how will they be overcome?**

INVESTOR'S PERSPECTIVE

Negative customer reactions to the company's product provide competitors with the opportunity to capture substantial market share at the company's expense. For example, during the earlier years of Ford Motor Company, competitors sensed customer dissatisfaction with Ford's policy of only offering one color—black. After capitalizing on this perceived weakness, competitors were able to capture a significant portion of Ford's industry-leading market share. The best defense against this occurrence is to encourage customer feedback actively while developing self-correcting internal systems.

6. **How will the company identify and contact prospective customers?**

INVESTOR'S PERSPECTIVE

Even if the company builds a better mousetrap, nobody will buy it if the company cannot identify or reach prospective customers. Available media vary from word of mouth and matchbox covers to national TV. If the company is cash poor but prefers to use national TV to market its product, investors will be discouraged by the obvious contradiction.

7. **What significant changes in the company's products/services are expected to be made over the next five to seven years (e.g., technology, styling, pricing, method of distribution)?**

INVESTOR'S PERSPECTIVE

Rather than waiting for competitors to develop significant breakthroughs, the company may believe that "the best defense is a good offense." However, smaller firms seldom have the financial resources to expend substantial dollars on research and development. The solution is greater research and development efficiency on the part of the smaller firms.

8. **Please discuss anticipated design and development problems with the company's products/services and management's approach to their solution.**

   INVESTOR'S PERSPECTIVE
   Besides jeopardizing the company's development program, problems could lead to significant time delays. The extent of management's preparation for anticipated problems will strongly influence investors.

9. **How will the company sell, finance and deliver its products/ services to foreign customers?**

   INVESTOR'S PERSPECTIVE
   Although foreign markets offer meaningful growth potential, most small business managers believe that they also involve countless obstacles. Investors prefer a management team that can accurately assess and capitalize on the opportunities that foreign markets offer the company.

E. General

1. **To what extent has management successfully presold the company's products/services? Include contracts, purchase orders, letters of intent, and other supporting documentation as an exhibit in appendix I.**

   INVESTOR'S PERSPECTIVE
   Advance contracts, letters of intent, and other indications of customer interest will significantly increase the company's chances of successfully raising growth capital.

VII. CUSTOMERS AND SUPPLIERS

A. Customers

1. **How many active customers does the company have, and how many of those active customers account for more than five percent of the subject company's total volume?**

Active Customers	Active Customers Accounting for More than 5% of Annual Volume

2. **If any customers representing more than five percent of the subject company's volume have been lost during the last three years, please explain why.**

    INVESTOR'S PERSPECTIVE
    High-volume customers can be both an asset and a liability. While the sales volume they generate may represent a major portion of the company's sales, a sudden change in customer loyalty could throw the company into an unprofitable position. Also, high-volume customers sometimes demand preferential treatment (e.g., price concessions, accelerated delivery) which results in substandard treatment of other customers. Again, investors prefer diversification over concentration.

3. **Please list the company's five largest customers including sales to each customer for both the last three years (actual) and the next three years (projected), percentage of company's total sales, credit rating (from one to ten, with ten representing the strongest rating), maximum credit extended, terms, length of purchasing history with subject company, and a brief description of each customer's business.**

    INVESTOR'S PERSPECTIVE
    Longer customer relationships indicate loyalty and stability while shorter relationships reflect the opposite. Major customers with marginal credit ratings are perceived as risk intensive because of their questionable ability to survive financial problems and pay their bills to the company in a timely manner if at all. Customers with marginal credit ratings should *not* be permitted to run up large balances owed to the company, even if the company must risk losing some of its major customers. A customer in a growth industry is a better future prospect than a customer whose total market is shrinking. A company is really only as strong as its customers.

    a. _____ _____
    Company   **Individual Contact**

    _____
    Address

    _____
    City, State

    _____ _____
    Phone   **Length of Purchasing History**

    _____ _____
    Credit Rating   **Maximum Credit Extended**
    TERMS:

                                            Actual

    Date of Fiscal Year End   ____ ____ ____

    Annual Sales to Customer   ____ ____ ____

Percentage of Subject
Company's Total Sales   ____   ____   ____

                                        Projected

Date of Fiscal Year End   ____   ____   ____

Annual Sales to Customer   ____   ____   ____

Percentage of Subject
Company's Total Sales   ____   ____   ____

DESCRIPTION OF BUSINESS:

4. **Please list the company's most promising prospective customers. Provide names of individual contacts, firm names, addresses, phone numbers, and estimated annual volume over the next three years with each prospect.**

   INVESTOR'S PERSPECTIVE
   To insure growth, the company must generate an updated list of quality prospects. If some of these prospects are not assured, the company must examine its weaknesses as perceived by the marketplace.

B. **Suppliers**

   INVESTOR'S PERSPECTIVE
   Investors look for a diversified group of quality suppliers since the company's production flow is directly dependent on its suppliers' ability to deliver. Suppliers can also provide inexpensive financing by extending terms to the company.

1. **Please list the company's five largest suppliers including approximate annual purchases from each supplier, maximum credit extended, and terms.**

   a. _____   _____
      Company   **Individual Contact**

      _____
      Address

City, State _____ Phone _____

Annual Purchases _____ Maximum Credit Extended _____
TERMS:

b. _____

Company _____ Individual Contact _____

Address _____

City, State _____ Phone _____

Annual Purchases _____ Maximum Credit Extended _____
TERMS:

c. _____

Company _____ Individual Contact _____

Address _____

City, State _____ Phone _____

Annual Purchases _____ Maximum Credit Extended _____
TERMS:

d. _____

Company _____ Individual Contact _____

Address _____

City, State _____ Phone _____

| Annual Purchases | Maximum Credit Extended |

TERMS:

e.

| Company | Individual Contact |

| Address | |

| City, State | Phone |

| Annual Purchases | Maximum Credit Extended |

TERMS:

2. **Please discuss the company's access to key raw materials and the steps that management has taken to protect the company from critical supply shortages.**

   INVESTOR'S PERSPECTIVE
   Management should both diversify its sources of supply and prepare contingency plans for shortages. For example, a company should not rely on one overseas supplier for a particular component because of potential political or transportation problems. Ideally, the company should have several different sources from several different parts of the world.

3. **Please discuss in detail any contracts now in effect with suppliers or any advance payments made to suppliers. Include copies of contracts and other supporting documentation as an exhibit in appendix I.**

   INVESTOR'S PERSPECTIVE
   The company should maximize its flexibility by avoiding supply contracts and advance payments unless cancellation without penalty is provided. However, supply contracts may be necessary to avoid price fluctuations or to assure delivery of scarce components.

VIII. PRODUCTION AND OPERATIONS

A. GENERAL

1. **Please describe the production process for each of the company's products/services. Include a flow chart, where applicable, that highlights the time frame and relationship of each step to the total operation, and other supporting documentation as an exhibit in appendix I.**

   INVESTOR'S PERSPECTIVE
   A flow chart should be used as a conceptual aid to give the investor a step-by-step overview of the production process.

2. **Please discuss the company's quality control system, the percentage of total units rejected versus units produced and the percentage of total units returned versus units produced for each product line over each of the last three years. What steps have been taken to improve the company's quality control system?**

   INVESTOR'S PERSPECTIVE
   Although somewhat neglected by American industry during the 1970s, quality control is now acknowledged to be of major importance. In addition to lost productivity

represented by rejection and returns, the company should consider the loss of customer goodwill and the cost of warranty service. The best marketing program will not offset poor quality control.

3. **Does the company fabricate a standard shelf-type product, manufacture to specification, or both?**

   INVESTOR'S PERSPECTIVE
   A standard shelf-type product will be more marketable and therefore carry a higher collateral value for financing purposes. Also, a shelf-type product will offer greater opportunities for automation. Because manufacturing to specification is a more specialized process, it usually carries a higher profit margin.

4. **What is the present capacity of the company's production facility in both dollar and unit volume versus its actual volume over each of the last three years. What percentage of capacity has been utilized for each of the last three years?**

   INVESTOR'S PERSPECTIVE
   Because the expansion of production facilities involves major capital expenditures, investors prefer the availability of additional productive capacity at minimal cost.

5. **How do the company's production facility and process compare with state-of-the-art technology? Please explain the proprietary aspects of the company's manufacturing process.**

   INVESTOR'S PERSPECTIVE
   If the efficiency of its manufacturing process provides the company with a cost and/or quality advantage, the company will have a superior strategic position over its competitors. If, however, the company must reach an ambitious sales level to pay for the costs of its manufacturing facility, it could find itself giving away its profit advantage to attract higher volume.

6. **Please discuss the company's safety record.**

   INVESTOR'S PERSPECTIVE
   If the company's safety record is not already excellent, management should explain steps that are being taken

to improve performance. Accidents reduce productivity, create liability, and damage employee morale.

7. **Please discuss the criteria that the company's management uses to determine whether products/services should be manufactured/performed in-house or purchased from another source.**

   INVESTOR'S PERSPECTIVE
   Manufacturing in-house affords management the opportunity to better control quality and assure supply. At certain volume levels, in-house manufacturing is also cheaper. However, purchasing from another source reduces fixed overhead and in some cases allows the company to concentrate on what it does most profitably.

8. **How will the company organize and operate its purchasing function to insure both an adequate supply of production materials and the best price and terms?**

   INVESTOR'S PERSPECTIVE
   Again, diversification and thorough preparation reduce risk.

B. Time constraints

1. **What is the length of the production cycle, in days, for each of the company's products/services?**

   DEFINITION
   Production Cycle—The amount of time required for the company to prepare its product for sale. Items such as liquor or livestock have long production cycles, whereas a newspaper has a short production cycle. The length of the cycle is influenced by the nature of the production process (e.g., aging of liquor must take several years), as well as by the availability of component parts necessary to complete the production process.

   INVESTOR'S PERSPECTIVE
   A shorter production cycle allows for rapid adjustment of production levels to sudden changes in market demand.

Longer cycles create vulnerability to fluctuations in the supply of vital materials. Therefore, investors perceive long production cycles as risk intensive.

2. **How and when will plant space and equipment be expanded to the capacities required by the company's sales projections? Please describe future equipment and construction needs along with cost and time estimates.**

   INVESTOR'S PERSPECTIVE
   The inability of the company to increase productive capacity at a reasonable cost and within a reasonable time frame, could severely stifle its growth. Forward planning is a must.

3. **How long must the company wait after placing an order for either new or replacement machinery and equipment?**

   INVESTOR'S PERSPECTIVE
   Production delays result in both lower sales revenue and the loss of customer goodwill. In some cases it is preferable to warehouse idle machinery and equipment than to risk serious future delays.

4. **Please prepare a month-by-month schedule that shows the timing and interrelationship of major events necessary for the company to realize its objectives (e.g., completion of prototypes, organization of sales/distribution network, receipt of first orders, first sales and deliveries, first collection of accounts receivable, first positive monthly cash flow, first profitable month of operation, completion of major additions to plant and equipment, final repayment of start-up debt).**

   INVESTOR'S PERSPECTIVE
   This exercise can help pinpoint critical events to which the company's resources should be committed. For example, if three events are scheduled simultaneously, but only one must be completed before subsequent steps can begin, then that event is a potential bottleneck or critical event.

5. **Please discuss the activities that are likely to cause a substantial delay in the company's development. What preventive**

steps will management take either to avoid or to minimize the impact of serious delays?

INVESTOR'S PERSPECTIVE
    The depth of the company's contingency plans will directly reflect on the quality of management.

IX. GOVERNMENT REGULATION

A. **Please list all licenses and government approvals that the company should receive or maintain in order to conduct its business. Include copies of licenses, approvals, and other supporting documentation as an exhibit in appendix I.**

INVESTOR'S PERSPECTIVE

Highly regulated areas are viewed as risk intensive by investors because of the unpredictable nature of political decision makers. For example, the synthetic fuel industry was strongly endorsed by the Carter administration. Accordingly, certain subsidies, tax benefits and incentives were offered to investors but were later withdrawn or modified. Investors who committed funds to synthetic fuel plants found themselves in a precarious position because of the government's change in attitude.

SOURCES

The company should begin investigating regulatory requirements by consulting with its attorney, local chamber of commerce, and branch offices of relevant federal agencies.

B. **Which city, county, state, and federal government agencies will**

the company be interfacing on a regular basis (e.g., EPA, EEOC, FDA, FTC, OSHA, SBA, SEC.)?

> *DEFINITIONS*
> *EPA*—Environmental Protection Agency
> *EEOC*—Equal Employment Opportunity Commission
> *FDA*—Food and Drug Administration
> *FTC*—Federal Trade Administration
> *OSHA*—Occupational Safety and Health Administration
> *SBA*—Small Business Administration
> *SEC*—Securities and Exchange Commission

C. Please discuss the problems that the company has encountered or anticipates encountering while attempting to comply with the above regulatory agencies.

> *INVESTOR'S PERSPECTIVE*
> If the company alienates one or more of the regulatory agencies, the repercussions could be extremely serious.

D. Please discuss proposed changes in the law (federal, state, and municipal) that could adversely affect the company. What steps has management taken to protect itself from unfavorable legislation?

> *INVESTOR'S PERSPECTIVE*
> Smaller companies are very vulnerable to changes in federal, state, and local laws. A contractor whose largest customer is the Department of Defense is vulnerable to changes in procurement legislation. Automobile emission systems manufacturers are vulnerable to EPA changes in antipollution standards. A small retailer is vulnerable to changes in the local zoning laws. Unlike larger companies, smaller firms do not have the resources to affect directly the political process. Thus, in addition to researching existing laws and regulations, the aspiring entrepreneur must also gauge the possibilities of and prepare strategic responses to dramatic changes in federal, state, and local laws.

X. FINANCIAL DATA

INVESTOR'S PERSPECTIVE
Comprehensive financial analysis can alert management to problems before they seriously damage the company. Cost and asset management are essential to the survival of a young, rapidly growing business. Authorities on small business management cite undercapitalization as the most frequent cause of small business failure. Thus strong financial management may increase the company's chances of survival by better allocating scarce cash flow.

A. Financial Operations

*1. What were/will be the company's sales, operating income (loss), net income (loss), and net after tax cash flow (deficit) for both the last three years (actual) and the next three years (projected)?

INVESTOR'S PERSPECTIVE
Net Income is a measurement of a company's performance for a given period but *Cash Flow* is the life blood of a

---

* For definitions of sales, operating income, net income, and net-after-tax cash flow, see page 67, section A.8.

small business. The company's bills and obligations are paid out of cash flow not net income. Certain <u>noncash</u> expenses (e.g., depreciation, deferred taxes) are deducted from revenues to determine net income but cash flow more accurately reflects the internal generation of funds available for payment of expenses and distribution to investors.

Management should explain all assumptions and supporting research used in the preparation of projections. Without detailed research and evidence of customer interest in the proposed venture, projections will have little, if any, credibility.

Actual

**Date of Fiscal
Year End** _____ _____ _____

Sales _____ _____ _____

**Operating Income
(Loss)** _____ _____ _____

Net Income (Loss) _____ _____ _____

**Net After-Tax Cash
Flow (Deficit)** _____ _____ _____

Projected

**Date of Fiscal
Year End** _____ _____ _____

Sales _____ _____ _____

**Operating Income
(Loss)** _____ _____ _____

Net Income (Loss) _____ _____ _____

**Net After-Tax Cash
Flow (Deficit)** _____ _____ _____

2. **What percentage of the company's total annual sales was/will be represented by lease revenues/foreign revenues for both the last three years (actual) and the next three years (projected)?**

Actual

**Date of Fiscal Year
End** _____ _____ _____

Lease Revenues _____ _____ _____

Foreign Revenues _____ _____ _____

Projected

**Date of Fiscal Year
End** _____ _____ _____

Lease Revenues _____ _____ _____

Foreign Revenues _____ _____ _____

3. **What is the company's present backlog versus its ending backlog for each of the last three fiscal years?**

    INVESTOR'S PERSPECTIVE
    A growing backlog is usually a positive indication of growing demand for the company's products/services. However, it can also be an indication of inadequate production or distribution capacity.

    Previous Three Years

    **Date of Fiscal Year
    End** _____ _____ _____

    Backlog _____ _____ _____

    Present

    Date Computed _____

    Backlog _____

4. **What is the minimum percentage of productive capacity that the company must utilize, the minimum sales volume it must generate, and the minimum market share it must ob-**

tain over each of the next three years to break even? Include both net income and cash flow breakeven analyses by product/service line and other supporting documentation as an exhibit in appendix I.

DEFINITIONS
   Breakeven Analysis—A method of assessing a firm's profit potential and downside risk. To perform this analysis, the firm's costs should be separated into variable components (e.g., labor, materials, sales commissions) and fixed components (e.g., interest expense, rent, managers' salaries, insurance, utilities). With these costs and the estimated selling price per unit, the company can estimate how many units of production must be sold to cover the costs of operation. At this sales volume, management incurs neither a loss nor a profit. Thus a comparison can be made between projected unit sales and the number of units that must be sold for the company to break even. If the company projects sales of 1000 units over the first year, but only requires sales of 500 units to break even, then the company has only to attain 50% of its projected volume to break even. The breakeven point is calculated with the following formulas:

Breakeven point (in units)
      = (Total Fixed Costs)
      /(Sales price per unit − Variable Cost per unit)

Breakeven point (in dollars)
      = (Breakeven point in units) × (Sales price per unit)

To illustrate the use of breakeven analysis, consider the following scenario:
   ABC Manufacturing produces a product that is sold for $10 per unit and that costs $5 per unit to manufacture. Fixed overhead is $20,000 per year. What is the breakeven volume in units?

Fixed Costs–$20,000
Contribution Margin per Unit–$10 − $5 = $5 per unit
Breakeven Volume = ($20,000)/($5 per unit) = 4000 units

A manager can use this analysis to illustrate the effects on the company's profitability of a price change, projected cost increases, or a reduction in demand (downside risk) and selling prices. The breakeven analysis is also a useful tool for forecasting the financial outcome of a new product introduction.

For example, assume that ABC Manufacturing is considering the introduction of a new product. The product costs ABC $2 per unit to produce. ABC will be able to produce a maximum of 40,000 units. The fixed overhead attributable to the introduction of this product will be $10,000. What should the minimum sales price of the product be?

(40,000 units) = ($10,000)/(Minimum Price-$2)
Minimum Sales Price = $2.25

Fixed Costs—Expenses that do not fluctuate with volume (dramatic increases in volume would eventually require an addition to productive capacity and associated fixed costs, while a sustained decrease in volume would cause management to liquidate some of its productive capacity). Although total fixed costs remain constant as volume increases, per-unit costs decrease. Fixed costs are usually divided into two categories: programmed costs and committed costs. Committed costs are those costs that are necessary to maintain the organization, e.g., rent, administrative salaries, interest, utilities, insurance. Programmed costs are expended with the objective of increasing sales, e.g., advertising, promotion, salesmen's base salary.

Variable Costs—Expenses that are uniform per unit of output. Total variable costs fluctuate in direct proportion to volume. They include direct materials, labor used in the production process, and salesmen's commissions.

Breakeven Analysis Based on Net Income

Date of Fiscal Year End	___	___	___
Capacity Utilization	___	___	___
Sales Volume	___	___	___
Market Share	___	___	___

Breakeven Analysis Based on Cash Flow

Date of Fiscal Year End	___	___	___

Capacity Utilization	___	___	___
Sales Volume	___	___	___
Market Share	___	___	___

Comparison of Projected Results to Breakeven Analysis

Date of Fiscal Year End	___	___	___
Sales Volume Required for Breakeven on a Net Income Basis	___	___	___
Sales Volume Required for Breakeven on a Cash Flow Basis	___	___	___
Projected Sales Volume	___	___	___
"Net Income" Break Even Sales Volume as a Percent of Projected Sales Volume	___	___	___
"Cash Flow" Breakeven Sales Volume as a Percentage of Projected Sales Volume	___	___	___

5. **What were/will be the company's expenditures for capital equipment, research and development, and advertising/promotion during both the last three years (actual) and the next three years (projected)?**

    DEFINITIONS
    Capital Equipment—Fixed assets used in the production of the company's goods and services (e.g., plant, equipment, machinery).

    Investor's Perspective—These items are viewed as elective expenditures that may divert scarce cash flow from payment of day-to-day operating expenses. However, some experts argue that reduction of expenditures on these elective items will damage that company's long-term growth prospects.

	Actual		
Date of Fiscal Year End	_____	_____	_____
Capital Equipment	_____	_____	_____
Research & Development	_____	_____	_____
Advertising/Promotion	_____	_____	_____

	Projected		
Date of Fiscal Year End	_____	_____	_____
Capital Equipment	_____	_____	_____
Research & Development	_____	_____	_____
Advertising/Promotion	_____	_____	_____

6. **Based on the following formula, please calculate the company's return on assets for both the last three years (actual) and the next three years (projected).**

$$\frac{\text{Year End Net Income}}{\text{Year End Total Assets}} = \text{Return on Assets}$$

INVESTOR'S PERSPECTIVE

This ratio is used to measure how productively management utilizes its assets. Comparisons are usually made in the following ways:

(1) The company's present performance versus previous performances.
(2) The company's projected performance versus present performance.
(3) The company's performance versus competitors' performance.
(4) The company's performance versus industry performance.

SOURCES
Robert Morris Associates (1616 PNB Building, Chestnut Street, Philadelphia, PA 19107; 215/665-2850) publishes financial statistics for virtually every industry by size.

	Actual		
Date of Fiscal Year End	_____	_____	_____
Return on Assets	_____	_____	_____

	Projected		
Date of Fiscal Year End	_____	_____	_____
Return on Assets	_____	_____	_____

7. **Based on the following formulas, please calculate the company's net income and cash flow returns on investment for both the last three years (actual) and the next three years (projected).**

$$\frac{\textbf{Year End Net Income}}{\textbf{Year End Net Worth}} = \frac{\textbf{Net Income}}{\textbf{Return on Investment}}$$

$$\frac{\textbf{Year End Cash Flow}}{\textbf{Year End Net Worth}} = \frac{\textbf{Cash Flow Return}}{\textbf{on Investment}}$$

DEFINITION
Net Worth—Also referred to as net book value and owner's equity. Equals total assets minus total liabilities.

INVESTOR'S PERSPECTIVE
Because investors are risking their capital in exchange for the promise of a substantial return, this figure is a very important indicator of what specific returns the investor can expect.

	Actual		
Date of Fiscal Year End	_____	_____	_____
Net Income Return on Investment	_____	_____	_____

**Cash Flow Return on
Investment** _____ _____ _____

                                        Projected

**Date of Fiscal
Year End** _____ _____ _____

**Net Income Return
on Investment** _____ _____ _____

**Cash Flow Return
on Investment** _____ _____ _____

8. **Please provide an analysis of unit sales, dollar sales, gross profit, gross margin, operating income (loss), operating margin, pretax income (loss), pretax margin, net income (loss), net margin, and net-after-tax cash flow by product/service line, territory, subsidiary, division, branch, etc., for both the last three years (actual) and the next three years (projected).**

    DEFINITIONS

        Sales—virtually all revenues received from customers in exchange for the company's goods and services minus discounts and/or returns.

        Cost-of-Goods-Sold (abbreviation COGS)—Direct costs incurred in the production of the company's goods/services (e.g., materials, manufacturing labor, depreciation of manufacturing machinery and plant, utilities used in the manufacturing process)

        Gross Profit—Sales minus COGS

        Gross Margin—COGS divided by sales

        Operating Income—Sales minus COGS, selling, general and administrative expense

        Operating Margin—Operating income divided by sales

        Pretax Income—Operating income plus/minus nonoperating income/expenses (e.g., interest income and expense)

        Pretax Margin—Pretax income divided by sales

        Net Income—Pretax income, plus extraordinary items and profits or losses from discontinued operations (net of applicable taxes), minus state and federal income taxes. Also referred to as net earnings and net profit.

        Net Margin—Net income divided by sales

        Net-after-tax cash flow—Net income plus non-cash expenses (e.g., depreciation, deferred taxes comma, loss on sale of equipment).

INVESTOR'S PERSPECTIVE

By breaking down the company's profit and loss statement into operating groups, the investor can isolate profitable divisions from losers. If a division has a history of losses, management should consider disposing of it rather than permitting it to "bleed" the company.

9. **If business is seasonal, please describe peaks in production, sales, employment, etc., and how they affect the company. What measures has management taken to offset the negative effects of seasonal fluctuations?**

INVESTOR'S PERSPECTIVE

Seasonal businesses must accumulate extremely large inventories in anticipation of high-volume seasons. If inventory is not large enough to meet demand, the company faces lost sales and profits that cannot be recaptured in the off season. If inventory exceeds demand, the company may not generate sufficient cash to pay suppliers and creditors. The company must absorb inventory carrying costs until surplus merchandise can be sold or disposed of. Because the company's financial performance is dependent on the outcome of the selling season, interim financial reports are distorted and in some cases virtually useless.

The best strategy to offset the negative aspects of a seasonal business is to acquire a counter-seasonal product line. For example, a lawn mower manufacturer could diversify into the snowmobile business. Diversification would hopefully even out the timing of the company's cash flow.

10. **Please discuss the design, installation, and maintenance of the company's cost and cash flow control systems. How often will data be collected and what actions will be taken to reduce costs that are found to be running in excess of projections?**

INVESTOR'S PERSPECTIVE

Cost and cash flow control systems allow management to detect variances between historical or projected results and actual results. Problems causing the variance can then be isolated and remedied before losses are permitted to accumulate. For example, if a particular machine has historically produced "widgets" at a direct cost of 3¢ per item, but cost control systems show a recent cost of 5¢ per item, management is alerted to the problem and can react accordingly. Further research into the problem might indicate a mechanical malfunction or improper use of the machine by a new employee.

11. **What are the available trade-offs between fixed and variable costs (e.g., can some of the full-time work force be replaced by part-time employees; can part of the manufacturing process be subcontracted to outside suppliers: can a short-term lease substitute for the purchase of a warehouse)? Include projected income statements, divided into fixed and variable cost component, for the next three years (i.e., monthly for the first year and quarterly for the second and third years), and other supporting documentation as an exhibit in appendix I.**

INVESTOR'S PERSPECTIVE
During periods of prosperity a company may attempt to reduce the overall cost-of-goods-sold by converting variable costs to fixed costs (e.g., a component may be manufactured internally rather than purchased from a supplier). During economic downturns, a company may follow the opposite strategy (e.g., reduce fixed expense by selling manufacturing capacity and purchasing components that were previously manufactured internally from outside suppliers). For a definition of fixed and variable costs, please see Chapter X, Section A.4.

12. **What are the company's most significant costs (e.g., energy, raw materials, freight, packaging, direct labor, interest on borrowed capital)? How volatile are they? And how does management propose to minimize their potential for having a negative impact on the company's profitability?**

INVESTOR'S PERSPECTIVE
By pinpointing significant costs, management can closely monitor those costs and prepare alternative strategies for different contingencies. For example, a candy maker may protect itself from a volatile cocoa market by hedging itself against rapid price increases through the commodity futures market. Escalating direct labor costs can be reduced over the long term by automating. Dramatic fluctuations in costs for certain supplies can be reduced through the negotiation of forward contracts and the diver-

sification of suppliers. Variable interest on borrowed capital can be replaced by a fixed interest charge or a stock offering. Freight costs can be minimized by exploring alternative methods (e.g., rail versus truck).

13. What is the company's cost position relative to the industry, and how well could it withstand prolonged price pressures from competitors?

INVESTOR'S PERSPECTIVE

As previously discussed, various factors affect the company's overall cost of delivering its product or service. If the company's cost is significantly higher than its competitors', a "price war" could force the company to price its product below its cost, or lose its customer base. Thus a prolonged period of price competition could deplete the company's capital base and force it into bankruptcy. To protect itself from this situation, the company must differentiate its product in many other ways. This will cause the consumer to consider such factors as quality, service, style, and durability, rather than price alone.

B. Financial Condition

INVESTOR'S PERSPECTIVE

Before investing in the company, investors will want to determine the tangible net book value of its assets. This figure represents the anticipated proceeds that its stockholders would receive by selling the company's assets on an orderly basis to interested buyers over a six-month period, after all liabilities have been paid. Therefore, the investor will subtract questionable assets such as past due accounts receivable and obsolete inventory from figures stated in the company's financial statements. The investor will also request a credible appraisal for the company's fixed assets. The "net" figure will establish the minimum value of the company. Also, the revised asset values will give the investor a good indication of the company's collateral value. Finally, account agings requested below will give the investor insight into the quality of the company's assets and the current status of its liabilities (e.g., if the company has not been meeting its obligations on a timely basis, its liabilities will become past due or delinquent).

1. **Please list uncollectible loans/accounts receivable which either are currently on the company's books or have been written off in the past three years.**

   DEFINITION
       Write-off—When an account receivable is deemed to be uncollectible, it is deducted as a loss.

   INVESTOR'S PERSPECTIVE
       Although uncollectible accounts receivable should be held to a minimum, the absence of write-offs may indicate a credit policy that is overly strict and therefore a deterrent to potential customers that buy from competitors with more lenient credit policies.

   Date of Statement: _____
   Original Booking Date of Loan/

Account	Name of Debtor	Amount
_____	_____	_____
_____	_____	_____
_____	_____	_____

2. **Please list the company's accounts receivables that are more than 90 days old.**

   INVESTOR'S PERSPECTIVE
       Usually the probability of collecting an account receivable decreases with age. After 90 days the collectibility of an account becomes "questionable" unless special terms are extended by the company.

   Date of Statement: _____

Name of Account	Amount	Days Old
_____	_____	_____
_____	_____	_____
_____	_____	_____

3. **Please list customer accounts that represent more than 10% of the company's total accounts receivable.**

   INVESTOR'S PERSPECTIVE
   Diversification is preferred over concentration. Should one of the company's major customers not be able to pay amounts owed to the company, the loss could be devastating. To reduce risk, exposure to any one customer should not exceed 10% of total receivables. However, if the company has its customer's financial statements or other assurances of its customer's financial strength, management may decide to deviate from this policy.

   Date of Statement: _____

Name of Account	Amount	Percent of Total Receivables
_____	_____	_____
_____	_____	_____
_____	_____	_____

4. **How much has the company reserved for bad debts over the last three years?**

   INVESTOR'S PERSPECTIVE
   The bad debt reserve should provide a cushion against write-offs.

Date of Fiscal Year End	_____	_____	_____
Amount of Bad Debt Reserve	_____	_____	_____

5. **Based on the following formula, please calculate the number of days it has taken/will take for the company's accounts receivable to turn during both the last three years (actual) and the next three years (projected)?**

$$\frac{\text{Year End Receivables}}{\text{Year End Sales}} \times 365 = \frac{\text{Days Receivables}}{\text{Outstanding}}$$

INVESTOR'S PERSPECTIVE
This formula is used to measure both the efficiency of the company's accounts receivable collection methods and the quality of its accounts receivable portfolio. Days receivables outstanding should not exceed 30 to 45.

Actual

Date of Fiscal Year End _____ _____ _____

Days Receivables Outstanding _____ _____ _____

Projected

Date of Fiscal Year End _____ _____ _____

Days Receivables Outstanding _____ _____ _____

6. **Based on the following formula, how many days has it taken/will it take for the company's inventory to turn during both the last three years (actual) and the next three years (projected)?**

$$\frac{\text{Year-End Inventory}}{\text{Year-End Cost of Goods Sold}} \times 365 = \frac{\text{Days Inventory}}{\text{on Hand}}$$

INVESTOR'S PERSPECTIVE
This figure is used to evaluate how effectively the company is managing its inventory. Robert Morris Associates figures are used to establish an industry range. A low figure relative to the industry reflects efficient inventory management and minimal carrying costs. However, a low figure could also reflect frequent product shortages. A high figure may indicate inefficient inventory management and excessive carrying costs. A high figure may also be attributable to the maintenance of a large inventory to serve customers better.

Actual

Date of Fiscal Year End _____ _____ _____

Days Inventory on Hand _____ _____ _____

		Projected	
Date of Fiscal Year End	_____	_____	_____
Days Inventory on Hand	_____	_____	_____

7. **How old is the company's inventory?**

   INVESTOR'S PERSPECTIVE
   Investors can gauge the marketability of the company's inventory by examining how long the inventory has been on hand. Older inventory is more likely to be obsolete or slow moving.

   Beginning Date of Aging: _____

	0–30 Days	31–60 Days	61–90 Days	More than 90 Days
Dollar Value of Inventory	_____	_____	_____	_____
Percent of Total Inventory	_____	_____	_____	_____

8. **Please list the following approximate values of the company's fixed assets.**

	Machinery & Equipment	Real Estate & Improvements
Cost	$_____	$_____
Book Value	$_____	$_____
Replacement Value	$_____	$_____
Orderly Liquidation Value	$_____	$_____
Amounts of Liens/Mortgages	$_____	$_____

   DEFINITIONS
   Book Value—Amount indicated in the company's financial statement.

Replacement Value—The present cost of acquiring a similar asset.

Orderly Liquidation Value—Estimated value that an asset will sell for over a six-month period.

Liens/Mortgages—A claim against an asset pledged as collateral for a loan.

9. **Please list dates and amounts of delinquent taxes and associated tax liens.**

   INVESTOR'S PERSPECTIVE
   Because the government is likely to pursue delinquent taxpayers vigorously, tax liens should be avoided at all costs. Investors perceive tax delinquency as an indication of the company's inability to handle its obligations.

Delinquent Taxes		Tax Liens	
Date	Amount	Date	Amount
_____	_____	_____	_____
_____	_____	_____	_____
_____	_____	_____	_____
_____	_____	_____	_____

10. **Please list the company's delinquent accounts, notes, and other obligations.**

    Date of Statement: _____

Amount	Name of Creditors
_____	_____
_____	_____
_____	_____
_____	_____

11. Please list the company's accounts payable that are more than 90 days old.

> *INVESTOR'S PERSPECTIVE*
> If the company's accounts payables exceed 90 days for other than disputed accounts, it is likely that the company is financing its working capital shortage at its suppliers' expense. This practice is not encouraged by investors.

Date of Statement: _____

Name of Account	Amount	Days Old
_____	_____	_____
_____	_____	_____
_____	_____	_____
_____	_____	_____
_____	_____	_____
_____	_____	_____

12. Based on the following formula, how many days has it taken/will it take for the company's accounts payable to turn during both the last three years (actual) and the next three years (projected)?

$$\frac{\text{Year-End Payables}}{\text{Year-End Cost of Goods Sold}} \times 365 = \frac{\text{Days Payables}}{\text{Outstanding}}$$

Actual

Date of Fiscal Year End	_____	_____	_____
Days Payables	_____	_____	_____

Projected

Date of Fiscal Year End	_____	_____	_____
Days Payables	_____	_____	_____

13. Please list the following information for both the last three years (actual) and the next three years (projected):

DEFINITIONS

Robert Morris Industry statistics should be used as a basis of comparison for all of the following figures:

Working Capital (current assets minus current liabilities)—Total assets that will be converted to cash within one year minus liabilities that will come due within one year. This figure represents the cash cushion that the company will have available to meet unforeseen circumstances.

Current Ratio (current assets divided by current liabilities)—This ratio is used as a measurement of liquidity. A current ratio of 2 to 1 is generally accepted as satisfactory.

Total Sales Divided by Working Capital—This ratio is used as a measurement of liquidity relative to sales.

Total Liabilities Divided by Net Worth—This ratio is used as a measurement of the company's leverage. Anything less than a 1 to 1 ratio indicates a sound financial position.

Actual

Date of Fiscal Year End	_____	_____	_____
Total Sales	_____	_____	_____
Current Assets	_____	_____	_____
Current Liabilities	_____	_____	_____
Current Assets Minus Current Liabilities	_____	_____	_____
Ratio of Current Assets Divided by Current Liab.	_____	_____	_____
Total Sales divided by the Total of Current Assets Minus Current Liab.	_____	_____	_____
Total Liabilities	_____	_____	_____
Net Worth	_____	_____	_____
Total Liabilities Divided by Net Worth	_____	_____	_____

	Projected		
Date of Fiscal Year End	_____	_____	_____
Total Sales	_____	_____	_____
Current Assets	_____	_____	_____
Current Liabilities	_____	_____	_____
Current Assets Minus Current Liabilities	_____	_____	_____
Ratio of Current Assets Divided by Current Liabilities	_____	_____	_____
Total Sales Divided by the Total of Current Assets Minus Current Liabilities	_____	_____	_____
Total Liabilities	_____	_____	_____
Net Worth	_____	_____	_____
Total Liabilities Divided by Net Worth	_____	_____	_____

14. **Based on the following formula, please calculate the company's quick ratio for both the last three years (actual) and the next three years (projected).**

> *INVESTOR'S PERSPECTIVE*
> This ratio is used to measure liquidity available on short notice relative to short-term liabilities. A ratio of 1 to 1 or greater is an indication of financial strength.

$$\frac{\text{Cash + Marketable Securities + Year End Accounts Receivable}}{\text{Year-End Current Liabilities}}$$

	Actual		
Date of Fiscal Year End	____	____	____
Quick Ratio	____	____	____
	Projected		
Date of Fiscal Year End	____	____	____
Quick Ratio	____	____	____

15. **What credit analysis procedures will the company follow both to screen and to monitor noncash customers?**

    INVESTOR'S PERSPECTIVE
    Well-thought-out credit control and analysis procedures are essential to holding accounts receivable write-offs to a minimum. Credit services and trade associations provide additional support to internal credit departments. The company's bank can also offer valuable credit information.

16. **Please discuss details of all major inventory adjustments (e.g., inventory write-ups or write-downs) made during the last three years.**

    INVESTOR'S PERSPECTIVE
    Inventory adjustments can dramatically reverse the company's profit position. They also indicate poor inventory control systems.

17. **Please describe the company's inventory control system (e.g., manual or computerized, frequency of physical inventories, method of inventory valuation).**

    INVESTOR'S PERSPECTIVE
    A quality inventory control system is essential to prevent inventory mismanagement, obsolescence, and theft. The cost of carrying surplus inventory during periods of high interest rates can severely deplete the company's financial resources.

18. **How does the company account for slow moving/obsolete inventory (e.g., write-down, write-off, carry at full cost)?**

    INVESTOR'S PERSPECTIVE
    The conservative approach should be taken. Marginal inventory should be written off.

19. **Please discuss the original amount and current valuation of advances to or investments in affiliates.**

    INVESTOR'S PERSPECTIVE
    Advances to or investments in affiliates are perceived as a potentially serious cash drain.

20. **Excluding real property, please list the company's major fixed assets (e.g., machinery, equipment, leasehold improvements). For each item provide the following: amount, type and date of last appraisal; description, age, condition and location; method of depreciation, historical cost, replacement cost, and net book value; method and terms of acquisition (e.g., operating lease, financing lease, cash purchase); current principal balance and terms of associated financing. Include copies of appraisals, leases, loan documents, and supporting documentation as an exhibit in appendix I.**

    INVESTOR'S PERSPECTIVE
    These data are required to establish the current value of the company's fixed assets and an inventory of its productive capacity.

21. **Please describe all real property owned or occupied by the company (e.g., plants, offices, warehouses, showrooms, retail space). For each item, provide the following: amount, type and date of last appraisal; location, zoning, number of square feet, number of floors, age, condition of structure and specifications of physical protection systems (e.g., sprinklers, burglar alarms, security personnel); method of depreciation, historical cost, replacement cost, and net book value; method and terms of acquisition (e.g., lease, land contract, seller mortgage, cash purchase); current principal balance and terms of associated financing; access to railroad sidings, highways, and other means of transportation; availability and quality of utilities and public services; proximity**

to customers and suppliers. Include copies of appraisals, leases, mortgages, and other supporting documentation as an exhibit in appendix I.

INVESTOR'S PERSPECTIVE
These data can be used to establish the current value of the company's real property and the potential borrowing power that its real estate holdings represent.

22. **Please discuss any "hidden assets" that do not appear on the company's balance sheet (e.g., lifo reserve, loss reserves, patents, lease contracts, mailing lists).**

DEFINITIONS
LIFO—Last-In, First-Out is an inventory costing method that assumes the last units purchased are the first units to be sold. The cost of goods sold consists primarily of the most recently added units. Ending inventory consists of older layers of inventory. During periods of inflation, when prices are rising, LIFO leads to higher reported expenses and lower reported earnings. Also, the company's balance sheet will reflect a lower inventory account than valuation under the FIFO method. This difference is referred to as "LIFO reserve." As a result of lower income recognition for tax purposes, LIFO provides a method of cash flow conservation during inflationary times.

FIFO—First In, First Out is an inventory costing method that assumes the first units purchased are the first units to be sold. The cost of goods sold consists primarily of older units, and the ending inventory consists of newer layers of inventory. During inflationary times, FIFO relative to LIFO results in lower inventory expense and higher net income. While the balance sheet more accurately reflects true inventory value, the company recognizes greater income, pays higher taxes, and therefore suffers a reduction in cash flow.

INVESTOR'S PERSPECTIVE
Certain intangible assets can be sold for substantial amounts that are not reflected on the company's balance sheet (e.g., a long-term lease for a very desirable property at 50% of market value). Management should include an estimate of the value of all intangible assets.

23. **Please explain all of the company's contingent liabilities (e.g., unfunded pension and profit-sharing commitments, guarantees, off balance sheet leases, warranties, conditional sales, return privileges—include return experience as a percentage of sales over the last three years, royalty/franchise/ license agreements, tax returns open for audit). For each item, approximate the company's maximum exposure and discuss action taken by management to minimize the ultimate liability.**

    DEFINITIONS
    Unfunded Pension and Profit-Sharing Commitments— Although not reflected on the balance sheet, the company is fully liable for all future benefits promised to employees.
    *Off Balance Sheet Leases—*Although the company must honor certain obligations (e.g., short-term operating leases), the liability is not included on the company's balance sheet.

    INVESTOR'S PERSPECTIVE
    All of the company's present and potential liabilities should be fully disclosed. Contingent liabilities can dramatically change the company's financial position. If the investor feels that management has attempted to hide any contingent liabilities, the company will be immediately eliminated from further consideration.

24. **Please explain unusual items not clearly identified in the company's financial statements.**

    INVESTOR'S PERSPECTIVE
    Regardless of the quality of a company's financial statements, certain issues are not discussed in adequate detail (e.g., pending litigation, major agreements). Investors prefer full disclosure of all relevant information.

XI. STRATEGIC PLANNING

A. What is the company's overall strategic plan? Provide a scenario that explains how and why the subject company will grow and prosper over the next three to five years.

DEFINITION

Strategic Plan—Explains where the company is, where it is going, and how it is going to get there. The strategic plan clearly identifies future objectives and goals such as market share, return on investment, and growth both in units sold and in dollar revenues. Along with a timetable for achieving these objectives, the strategic plan must identify all critical risks or obstacles that may prevent their achievement. Because most aspiring entrepreneurs avoid the time-consuming process of planning, preferring instead to confront problems as they occur, these problems often prove fatal to the firm. However, if the entrepreneur anticipates problems before they occur and prepares effective contingency plans, the severity of those problems can be reduced. In some cases, certain problems can be prevented altogether.

INVESTOR'S PERSPECTIVE

The strategic plan should bring together and coordinate all subject matter examined in the business plan. It should explain how the different departments of the company will combine efforts to execute the strategic plan. Here's a hypothetical example. Say a company decided to establish itself as the industry leader (control the largest market share); it could raise capital through its finance department to purchase the most efficient plant and equipment available. Lower per unit cost combined with improved quality control would allow the company to increase market penetration. As the company grows, it will require additional management personnel through its recruitment and training program. Additional cash flow will provide funding necessary to increase its advertising effort which will in turn increase sales volume. Higher volume will permit the company to achieve maximum per unit efficiency, lower costs, and increase profits. As profits grow, the company will attract investor interest and eventually go public, yielding impressive returns to the original investors.

B. In order of importance, please discuss the critical risks, problems, and obstacles associated with the company, and how management plans to minimize the impact of unfavorable developments in each critical area (e.g., management inexperience, competitive price cutting, potentially unfavorable industry-wide trends, operating budget overruns, lower than projected sales volume, delays in product/service development, difficulties or delays in the procurement of raw materials, capital shortages, higher than expected research and development expenditures due to competitive pressures, excessive government regulation).

INVESTOR'S PERSPECTIVE

Identifying and preparing for potential problems are the most effective ways to "manage" risk. For example, the company can compensate for management inexperience by electing directors with extensive industry experience. Price cutting, and lower than projected sales, can be partially offset by a budget austerity program including employee layoffs and reduced advertising expenditures. Inadequate research and development programs can be supplemented with licensed technologies. Raw material shortages can be avoided by diversifying sources. It should be noted that many problems do not have simple or painless solutions. For example, the tripling of oil prices by the OPEC nations created monumental problems that few corporate planners anticipated. Similar to other aspects of business management, strategic planning is more of an art than a science.

C. What steps will management take to sustain the company's growth? Please describe the company's program for researching, developing, analyzing, and exploiting new opportunities.

> *INVESTOR'S PERSPECTIVE*
> The company that stops growing usually dies. One of the most compelling arguments for sound strategic planning is the possibility of identifying new growth opportunities for the firm. This is accomplished by recognizing unfulfilled customer needs to which the firm can bring to bear certain specialized skills, thereby gaining a competitive edge. Often, the firm must look outside the narrow product class with which it is familiar, and must identify the broader market need being served by the product. If this process is followed, the firm avoids the danger of being supplanted by another firm that more expeditiously perceives and reacts to a market opportunity through the application of a newer technology. For example, it would be of little value to become the dominant manufacturer of buggy whips at the same time that automobiles achieve consumer acceptance. Railroad companies are being supplanted by air transportation companies because railroad management ignored the full potential of a promising new technology. Thus, effective strategic planning is essential to the long-term prosperity of the firm.

D. How does management expect the US economy to perform over the next three to five years (e.g., recession/depression, real growth, interest rates, unemployment, inflation)?

> *SOURCES*
> The federal government compiles key economic statistics on a regular basis that are published in the Wall Street Journal and the business sections of local newspapers.

> *INVESTOR'S PERSPECTIVE*
> Due to the impact of the US economy on industry, management should prepare strategies for different economic

scenarios. The volatility of the economy over the last five years has emphasized the need for this type of planning.

E. How vulnerable is the company's profitability to cyclical fluctuations in the economy (e.g., changes in the rates of real growth, interest, inflation)? How will management protect the company from the negative consequences of economic volatility?

DEFINITION

Changes in the state of the US economy are usually explained in terms of cyclical downturns (weakening) or cyclical upturns (strengthening). Basically, the economy presents numerous variations of the same boom and bust cycle. Since each stage is associated with certain economic characteristics, it is in management's best interests to prepare a variety of economic strategies. For example, near the top of the economic cycle, interest rates climb and demand starts dropping. Accordingly, management should reduce inventories in an effort to minimize interest expense and carrying charges. Near the bottom of the economic cycle, interest rates continue to drop and demand begins to climb. In this case, the opposite strategy applies.

INVESTOR'S PERSPECTIVE

Investors prefer a management team that both understands and prepares for the frequent economic fluctuations that have characterized the US economy over the last five years.

XII. APPENDIXES

1 SUPPORTING DOCUMENTATION

Please include the supporting documentation specifically requested in the following questions:

I. Background

    A. General

    B. Legal

        10. Insurance policies

        7. Structural chart

        8. Franchise, royalty, license, working agreements, etc.

II. Management

    A. Organization chart

    F. Letters of recommendation

VI. Market & Competition

    C. Market Definition

        1. Market surveys, test market results, feasibility studies, trade association reports, government market data, etc.

E. General

1. Contracts, purchase orders, letters of intent, etc.

VII. Customers & Suppliers

B. Suppliers

3. Suppliers' contracts

VIII. Production & Operations

A. General

1. Production flow chart

IX. Government Regulation

A. Licenses, approvals, etc.

X. Financial

A. Financial Operations

4. Net income and cash flow breakeven analyses by product/service line
12. Projected income statements, divided and variable cost components, for the next three years (i.e., monthly for the first year and quarterly for the second and third years)

B. Financial Condition

20. Appraisals, leases, and loan documents
21. Appraisals, leases and mortgages

2 ADDITIONAL EXHIBITS

A. Historical consolidating financial statements for last five years (preferably audited).

B. Tax returns for the last five years.

C. Sales and pretax income by quarter over the last two years.

D. Interim financial statements, including a summary of recent developments.

E. Current aging of accounts receivable.

F. Current aging of accounts payable.

G. A full set of pro forma financial statements for the next three years, including income and cash flow statements (monthly breakdown for the first year and quarterly for the second and third years), balance sheets (semiannually for the first year and annually for the second and third years), and all relevant notes and assumptions.

H. Copies of the company's pension, profit-sharing, and stock bonus plans.

I. Personal financial statements of principal stockholders and guarantors.

J. Resumes of all individuals involved in the management of the company including directors, officers, and major shareholders (10% or greater interest in the subject company).

K. The subject company's last stock offering memorandum.

L. A list of the company's sales representatives, distributors, wholesalers, etc.

M. The company's current price lists, catalogs, brochures, product illustrations, and other promotional materials.

N. Miscellaneous information (newspaper and magazine articles, credit reports, competitor's annual reports, etc.).

Applicant represents and certifies the foregoing information, and that contained in attached schedules, to be true, correct, and complete and that said information is submitted to induce the addressee to advance funds to the applicant.

Part Two

Transforming Your Answers Into the Business Plan

INTRODUCTION

What follows are two business plans that were developed using the question and answer format provided in *How to Raise Capital*. Although the two businesses—a retail computer shop called Microland and a heating and air conditioning supply service called Complete Supply—are in many ways typical of those kinds of enterprises, the reader should be aware that the specific businesses themselves are fictitious. All the statistical and financial information provided about those businesses is also fictitious. THE READER SHOULD ALSO BE AWARE THAT THE BUSINESS PLANS PRESENTED HERE ARE NOT MEANT TO BE USED AS A PROGRAM FOR STARTING SUCH BUSINESSES, NOR ARE THEY DESIGNED TO RAISE CAPITAL FOR THOSE SPECIFIC BUSINESSES. The plans are included solely to illustrate the concepts discussed in this book. They are included in this book to give the reader a more concrete idea of how to transform the workbook portion of the text into a readable and effective business plan.

* * *

As mentioned in the introduction, it would be unwise to submit to prospective investors simply a series of questions and answers based on the format of this book. Although the questions provided in *How to Raise Capital* address all the pertinent issues, answering the questions

93

alone will not give an investor what he or she really needs to evaluate a business, namely, a synthesis and analysis of the material that the workbook section of this book helps you to generate.

The next section is organized into three parts. The first part consists of answers to the workbook questions for the company Complete Supply Service. These answers follow the same order as the workbook questions. The second part is a business plan for Complete Supply written from the material contained in the answers to the questions. The third part is a business plan for Microland.

You will notice that both business plans do not exactly follow the order of the workbook itself. This is intentional. The workbook portion of the text is meant as a guide for you to generate material to write your business plan. You should not feel compelled to follow the exact order of the questions in the workbook. Indeed, you may find it essential to put your discussion of Strategic Planning (Part XI in the workbook) before Marketing and Competition (Part VI in the workbook).

Synthesis and analysis are important here. Because most investors are inundated with business proposals, you must put the most important information about your venture at the beginning of your business plan. Like any piece of good writing, your business plan must "hook" your reader with the most significant facts and ideas as soon as possible. It's up to you to analyze and synthesize those important facts and ideas.

What are the significant facts and ideas about a business? Obviously, these facts and ideas depend on the business. There are no hard and fast rules you can apply. For a start-up operation, Strategic Planning is crucial: without an adequately thought-out strategic plan, the venture is doomed. An investor will want to know precisely what your strategic plan is. So for the business plan of a start-up, Strategic Planning should probably assume a prominent place. In the business plan for Microland—a start-up operation—a discussion of the venture's Strategic Plan comes immediately after the Overview. That position befits the importance of a strategic plan for Microland.

What seems eminently appropriate as an organizational principle for one venture's business plan, however, may be inappropriate for another venture's business plan. For example, you may have a product that no one else has, a product you are certain has overwhelming economic justification. Clearly, then, the section on Market and Competition is of paramount importance. That section should probably come immediately after the Overview. You perhaps should take certain sections of that portion of the workbook—such as Social and Behavioral

Characteristics of the Company's Customers (VI C, 6)—and develop them into major headings in your business plan, to emphasize their importance.

Consequently, the options for organizing your business plan are numerous indeed. Are you starting an investment management firm? Then the section on Management is crucial to a prospective investor, and the material that you develop from that portion of the book should be given a prominent position. Do you have a proprietary interest in a new, highly efficient, manufacturing process for a product already on the market? Then the section on Production and Operations must be developed fully and probably deserves a place at the beginning of your business plan.

But although numerous options exist for organizing your business plan, certain elements of the plan are not optional. Below is a list of those elements you must include in your business plan:

1. *Table of Contents.* Some investors are immediately interested in a business's management; they believe they invest as much in people as they do in products or ideas. Thus providing a table of contents will allow the investor to locate quickly the part that deals with management's qualifications, or any other aspect of the business that he considers important.

2. *An Overview,* or an Introduction. Most investors will decide to continue reading the business plan only if the introductory material arouses their interest. You should devote considerable time and energy writing an overview that explains precisely why your business is worth investing in—what makes it unique and sets it apart from the competition—in effect, why your business is or will be profitable. The overview should also tell the investor how much money you want, in what form (debt or equity), and what you intend to use it for (purchase of new plant or equipment, adding to inventory, or geographical expansion). Add a few sentences about the qualifications of management, and then refer the reader to the section on management.

3. *Explanation of Risks.* Every business has risks. Hence, every business plan should explain what risks exist for that business. If you don't know what the risks are, you do not know your business, and an investor will reject your business plan outright.

4. *Ways to Solve Risks.* Only pinpointing the specific risks of your business is not enough. You must show the potential investor that you have thought about solutions to those risks.

5. *Strengths and Weaknesses of Management.* An investor wants to see a realistic self-evaluation on the part of management.

6. *Ways Management Exploits Its Strengths and Minimizes Its Weaknesses.* Again, this shows the investor that solutions to the problems have been considered.

7. *Evidence to Back Up Assertations.* If you say the market for your product is $100 million, you need to provide evidence for that assertion. Who has given you that information? How reliable is that source?

8. *Explanation of the Product or Service.* You must tell potential investors exactly what your product or service is.

9. *Unique Selling Propositions.* What makes your product or service unique? Why will someone buy it?

10. *Discussion of the Market.* Who is going to buy your product? What are the characteristics of those people that make them want to buy your product? How large is the market now? How large will it be? How fast will it grow? What is your market share now? What will your market share be in the future, and why?

11. *Competition.* Who competes against you? What are the strengths and weaknesses of the competition? What are your strengths and weaknesses compared to theirs? Who will be your competition in the future? How do you plan to meet their challenges?

12. *Specifics.* Telling the investor, for example, that your business will increase its customer base by word of mouth isn't enough. You must focus on the specific ways you will encourage the spreading of your reputation. You might have incentive discounts for customers to bring in new prospects. You might have a well-planned policy to attend relevant association meetings in your area. Other possibilities should be considered.

13. *Financial Statements.* The best written business plan will be tossed aside by investors if you do not have well-prepared financial statements. Chapter X of the workbook has definitions and formulas for the statements you will need to generate. You can find more detail on these issues by referring to the relevant sections in Part One.

14. *Assumptions Behind Your Financial Statements.* Explain how you generated the projected financial profile of your company. How quickly will your inventory turn? How fast will your accounts be paid? If you are raising capital for a start up, what expenditures willl you have to make before you open your

doors? These are but a few of the assumptions you may have to address when developing your financial statements.

A Note on the Two Versions of the Complete Supply Service Business Plan

Some of the material contained in the final, written version of Complete Supply's Business Plan is not contained in the answers to the workbook questions. You will probably find the same situation when you assemble your business plan. Why? In the process of reworking the material from the questionnaire to the final written business plan, you will probably reevaluate your answers, and this reevaluation may lead you to add significant material that may have been left out. You may entirely reword certain sections to explain more clearly what your business is and how it operates. In some cases, you may even eliminate material that you decide is superfluous or redundant.

That is what happened when the Complete Supply Service business plan was generated. One of the authors purposely composed rough draft answers to the questions contained in Part One. Another author wrote the final version of Complete Supply's Business plan based on the answers to the workbook questions.

But more happened to produce the final version than merely reassembling the answers to the workbook questions. The process of coming to the final version was a dynamic one. Questions answered cursorily were explored in greater detail. The two authors worked together, generating more evidence and more specifics. For example, the answers to questions from the section on Marketing and Competition were expanded considerably to produce the final written version. The organizational structure of the final business plan also underwent many changes.

The changes that resulted from this dynamic process are too numerous to mention here. However, what happened here will probably happen to you when you produce your own business plan. Of course, you could answer the workbook questions thoroughly and completely, and have relatively few changes to make when you write your final, prose version. (At the very least, you'll have to provide transitions between paragraphs and sections of your prose version).

No matter what tactical approach you take, the workbook portion of *How to Raise Capital* is designed to make you think thoroughly about all the essential issues affecting your business. And the process of transforming the workbook answers into a prose version should make you think even harder about your business. If this happens when you produce your business plan, you have derived all the benefits this book can give.

*   *   *

What follows immediately is the workbook version of Complete Supply's business plan. It contains answers to the questions outlined in the first part of *How to Raise Capital*. Answering these questions generated much of the information needed to write the completed prose version of the business plan, which is presented directly after the answers to the workbook version. If the questions had been answered thoroughly, they would have supplied all the material needed for the final plan; however, Complete Supply's workbook answers overlooked some significant information. Thus, at the end of some of the answers, the reader will find, in parentheses, comments about the quality of the answer and the need for additional material. These comments will be preceded by the phrase "What's needed," and will point out only the most significant omissions in the answers. Every necessary change is not detailed. To show how the remaining changes were made, the authors encourage the reader to compare carefully the two versions of Complete Supply's business plan.

Please note that throughout the workbook section you will find many asterisked questions. This designation was used to indicate the answers to these questions, along with required charts, are provided in the written version of Complete Supply's Business Plan. Rather than duplicating certain exhibits or answers, we used this method to demonstrate best how this book should be used.

WORKBOOK QUESTIONS

ANSWERED FOR

Complete Supply Service

I. BACKGROUND

A. Overview

Complete Supply Service is a company that offers heating and air conditioning supplies to the Chicago market. Its customers are primarily service companies and contractors that recognize the quality, service, and price that Complete Supply provides.

The company was founded in 1965 by a small group of individuals who had left their previous jobs in an effort to gain the independence and rewards, both monetary and psychic, that operation of an independent company can offer. The principals of Complete Supply Service Company are Jean Winklereid, Sekhar Bahadur, Charles Bobrinskoy, and Eric Kuby. The company is located on the south side of Chicago. The company's offices and warehouse are located near several major highways.

Sales typically peak in the middle of the summer for air-conditioning products and in the middle of winter for heating products. Typical sales items range from full-sized air conditioners for mid-sized apartment buildings to small nuts and bolts.

The company has been able to fare much better than its competitors because it bought large amounts of inventory in the off season to be resold during peak seasons. For example, the company purchased the appropriate amount of heating inventory during the summer to meet projected winter volume. While this strategy was somewhat risky, it was more profitable than its competitors' practice of buying during the peak season.

The higher level of sales anticipated for next summer season will require a substantial increase in inventory. Complete Supply is currently unable to purchase these inventories from current cash flow and an existing $200,000 revolving line of credit, and is seeking to acquire an additional short-term loan or a line of credit from a local bank. Because the principals enjoy sole ownership of the firm, they are unwilling to give up an equity position to investors. If the company receives the requested bank credit, then the profits realized from projected sales would place Complete Supply Company in a position to consider opening an additional warehouse on the north side of Chicago. (What Overview needs: specific information about the market; why sales will increase; the amount of financing Complete Supply requires; market niche; specific numbers associated with growth—for example, how much gross annual sales will increase once financing is in place).

    1. October 20, 1982

2. Complete Supply Service, Inc.

3. 3141 South Morgan Avenue, Chicago, Ill 60608

4. 523-0200

5. 1965

6. Accountant: Voila, Ross & Associates

7. The company originally sold only heating supplies that varied from medium to lower priced items. Typically, the company sold safety controls for boilers, air ducts, pipe, motors, fans, pumps, thermostats, and thermocouplers. The product line encompassed everything that the serviceperson might need for a service call. Often, a person will make a service call not realizing what the problem is. Upon inspection of the customer's heating unit, he/she might isolate the difficulty in a defective part. Without the part on hand, he/she would purchase the product from us. We later added air conditioning products with the same philosophy in mind.

As we grew, we were able to cut our prices on both lines by purchasing inventory during the off season. With the additional profits, we then began stocking major items, items that the serviceperson would usually purchase before going on service calls. These items included boilers and air conditioners for installation. We still do not stock larger heating units and air conditioners because the firms that install such units are able to purchase direct from the factory and because such very large items tend to tie up capital and turn over very slowly.

8. Because most of our customers are local customers who perform service calls in the area, we could probably raise prices without fear of losing their business. Hence, we enjoy a local monopoly in the supply business. Companies wishing to enter the market would have a difficult time competing simply because we enjoy a solid reputation, a large inventory, and knowledgeable support staff. In the larger Chicago-area market, we are able to compete with other supply houses because of our low prices.

Servicepeople who service other areas of the city often stock up on their inventories when they visit us. Our position in the industry enables us to purchase from major manufacturers at a discount even during peak season. Emerging supply houses would be unable to secure such discounts from manufacturers.

Inventory obsolescence is low. Boilers have a relatively long life, and hence demand for our inventories is consistent. Unlike the case of automobiles, heating and air conditioning parts are not restyled to promote obsolescence. Any inventory that might become rapidly obsolete, i.e., computerized thermostats, are purchased with the right of return to the manufacturers. Most servicepeople prefer familiar products and would rather install a part they have worked with before than a new part, even if the new part is superior and would render the old part obsolete.

9. If we are able to secure financing, we will be able to purchase larger quantities of inventory at greater discounts that can be passed on directly to the customer.

10. All of our officers are insured. The company would receive compensation for lost expertise. The buildings and inventories are fully covered by a variable policy that scales payments to the level of inventory. We pay a premium for such a policy, which we feel is warranted when one considers the potential loss. (What's needed: more specifics about the policies in effect—the type of insurance, extent of the premium, and so on.)

11. Our company is close to several major highways. This is beneficial since most of our initial customers bought from us because of our proximity to their work site. Our Chicago location is a benefit since we are able to draw upon a large pool of labor. The disadvantage of our south side location is that we lose potential north side business to local north side supply houses. However, if Complete Supply implements the major elements of its long-term strategic plan—expanding to the north side—we will be in a better position to compete in that area of the city.

12. Official housing start records, sales history of our major suppliers, profitability of similar companies, local servicemen, number of dwellings in the south side, etc. (What's needed: Information about projected housing starts, statistics about the resale market; citation of authoritative sources for this information).

B. Legal

1. Corporation
2. Illinois
3–9. n/a

II. MANAGEMENT

A. Charlie Bobrinskoy, president, 45. Engineer from Heat-Me, a major manufacturer of heating and air conditioning units. Very familiar with the industry. The son of a boiler serviceman.

Jean Winklereid, Vice President and Director of operations. 47. Founding member. Previously an officer for a large clothing store. Base salary of $40,000 plus 25% of bonus. Owns 25% of company.

Very Knowledgeable in dealing with suppliers, establishing inventory levels, forecasting projected sales.

Sekhar Bahadur, Vice President and Chief Financial Officer, 46. Worked previously as CFD for Salosachs, a local real estate investment firm. Strong in structuring financing. Effective at preparing budgets and evaluating investments—additional outlets, decisions involving whether to carry a specific line of goods.

Eric Kuby, Vice-President and Director of Marketing, 44. Worked previously for Jewel Food Stores in their marketing department.

(What's needed for Question A: salary and profit-sharing specifics, more about educational and career accomplishments, specific responsibilities for the company.)

B. The goals of all of the directors are to establish a very profitable company. All officers wish to continue private ownership of the firm.

C. All officers are directors.

D. Before forming Complete Supply Company, each member of management was successful in his or her various field. All of the various divisions of the firm are directed by talented persons familiar with the field and their responsibilities. (What's needed: more detail about managements' weaknesses; also, what particular responsibilities each member of management has.)

E. n/a

F. Viola, Ross and Associates, accountants.
Steinman, Markowitz, Brown, Brown and Brown, lawyers.
Exchange National Bank, Mr. David Rudes.
American National Bank. Ms. Mary Rudes.
First National Bank. Mr. Clay Rose.
First City, Mr. Michael Jurkash, Management Consultant.
Mount McKinsey and Associates, Ms. Rose Lyon, Management Consultant.

All of the above are business acquaintances and consultants. (What's needed: title and function of each of individuals at the firms listed as references and consultants.)

G. See above

H. Complete Supply Company is currently training several junior employees in each area of responsibility to take over management of the existing operation ultimately, thus allowing the principals to focus on long-range goals. Management trainees are placed in an apprenticeship program in which they are given a large degree of freedom to make their own decisions. All are performing exceedingly well.

I.–J. n/a

K. All employees receive salaries and profit-sharing packages that exceed compensation offered by competitors. The company's generous compensation program also greatly reduces the attraction of leaving to start a competitive business.

III. OWNERSHIP

A. All stock is equally divided among the four partners.

B. n/a

C. n/a

D. The company's stock bears a legend stating that it cannot be freely traded without complying with certain securities laws.

E. The company has purchased insurance on the lives of each of the principals. In the event of a principal's death, this insurance will provide the company with sufficient funds to purchase the stock of the deceased principal. The principals also have rights of first refusal regarding the sale of the company's stock to third parties.

F. The company's stock does not have cumulative voting rights.

G. n/a

IV. EMPLOYEES

A. *

B. Roughly 50% of the company's full-time employees will be skilled. All of the part-time help is unskilled.

C. None

D. *

E. Because of the abundant labor pool of both skilled and unskilled workers, we have no problem hiring new workers or replacing unsatisfactory ones. This is true for both full- and part-time workers.

F. All employees are entitled to paid vacations depending on number of years worked. One week paid for every two years worked until an employee has reached ten-years service. Employees have a maximum of five vacation weeks per year. Each employee receives one week of unpaid vacation per year. We offer a basic optional health medical plan.

G. Salary for skilled and unskilled workers is competitive.

H. We do require skilled employees to work the order desk. They answer customers' questions and identify parts a customer might need. Most of these employees are former servicepersons who left the field for various reasons. We have had no problem hiring employees with the required level of experience.

I. We enjoy a productive working relationship with our employees. They are paid competitively, and these hard working employees are justly rewarded with above average compensation. (What's needed: addressing the issue of work stoppage.)

J. Our sales force can be adjusted to sales volume, but we do not do so. In periods of low volume, we shorten employees' hours, schedule employees to take vacation, and perform inventory checks or maintenance work.

K. Our unskilled labor turnover is relatively high compared to that of our skilled turnover. Unskilled labor usually performs manual tasks such as maintaining stock and filling orders. Average employment is roughly 2.5 years. Our skilled labor turnover is lower. We lose about one person for every four years of work.

L. We do not have a formal training program for unskilled workers. We simply pair a new worker with a seasoned worker for a few days. Skilled workers are for the most part already trained for their position and are required only to learn the company's paperwork procedures.

V. INVESTMENT CRITERIA

A. General

1. Zero
2. 10,000 shares authorized, 1000 issued.
3. The principals are willing to provide personal guarantees of $50,000 each, for a total of $200,000.

4. Proceeds will be used to finance the purchase of additional inventories.

5. We have borrowed from all the banks listed in question IIF. Currently, the company's only outstanding debt is a $200,000 revolving credit line with Exchange National Bank, at 2.5% above prime, floating. Borrowed funds are used to cover normal purchases of inventory but are inadequate to cover forecasted purchases. This revolving line of credit is secured by a first lien on inventory and accounts receivable.

6. All of the banks listed in question IIF will be approached for the requested loan.

B. Terms

1. An additional $200,000.
2. Debt only.
3. The company will draw down the entire line throughout most of the year.

VI. MARKET AND COMPETITION

A. Market

1. Locally, yes. In the Chicago area we are roughly fifth. (What's needed: more specific information about the geographical size of the local and overall Chicago markets. Need authoritative sources to back up these assertions.)
2. See VI A.1.

B. Competition

1. *
2. Bob Mason is the only other firm that we believe to be better capitalized than our company. Most of the sales generated by the other firms can be attributed to the convenience of their locations to customers. The smaller supply houses are unable to match the volume purchase discounts of the major houses. Gregorious has a reputation for superior service; it offers on-the-job delivery service for even small-purchase items.

However, none of the above firms purchases during the off season as aggressively as we do. Our competition prefers not to carry off-season inventory. Our carrying several lines of parts as exclusive Chicago dealers gives us a significant edge over our competition.

3. n/a

C. Market Definition

1. Currently, the total Chicago-area market is estimated to be $40 million dollars. Next year, we predict it will increase to roughly $45 million and within the next five years to $65 million. A large number of gas boilers were installed in the early 1970s after passage of EPA laws made coal-burning heaters impractical. We forecast that most of these heaters will be experiencing breakdowns, causing increased demand for both replacement parts and new units. Market size over the past several years has remained relatively stagnant at $40 million. Another component of the estimated increase in market size to $65 million will be the consumer acceptance of heat pumps and energy-efficient air conditioners. (What's needed: authoritative sources for this information.)

2. South side of Chicago.

3. Because of the necessity of replacing defective parts, we enjoy a relatively assured demand for our parts. During periods of prosperity, people tend to install boilers while in other times they purchase parts to repair them. Also, energy conservationists advocate the frequent maintenance and repair of heating and air conditioning systems.

4. 1. Proximity
   2. Low price for high quality parts
   3. Support staff (behind the counter order-takers)
   4. Credit terms for good customers
   5. Large inventory ensuring good order fill

5. The need to purchase a part at a low price from a supplier that will probably have the part in stock.

6. Our customers are profit-oriented. They want to spend most of their time on a job where they can charge for their services rather than time hunting for a critical part. They also want quality parts so they won't have to reinstall a new part that has proven to be defective.

7. Continual feedback from our order fillers allows us to monitor the attitude of our customers. If they are unhappy with a product, or if they would like us to supply a product we don't currently carry, we will consider the appropriate changes.

8. We anticipate a larger number of servicepeople becoming affiliated with larger companies. Hence we are currently attempting to attract larger customers.

D. Market Strategy

1. Our best marketing medium is word of mouth. Servicepersons are a heterogeneous group that are hard to reach. From time to time, we rent booths at trade shows, but word of mouth seems to be the most effective method of spreading our reputation. Hence we offer incentives for customers to bring in new customers. We advertise to the large customer the same way we advertise to the serviceperson: low prices, quality products, high fill rate, solid support staff, and good credit terms. (What's needed: more thorough description, with specifics, of market strategy.)

2. See above, VI B, 2.

3. We could lose some cost advantage if competitors begin purchasing inventory during the off season as we do. However, only Mason has the warehouse space that is required to stock off-season inventory. We believe that that company lacks the financial and management expertise to follow this strategy. Even if Mason had the resources to emulate our strategy, we would continue to benefit from our local "monopoly." The other houses rely on high inventory turnover.

4. A major competitive breakthrough would occur if firms in areas of metropolitan Chicago served by our company were to build additional warehouse capacity in order to take advantage of off-season purchasing. We plan to protect ourselves from this possibility by establishing ourselves in other areas of the city as quickly as possible. With our established name and reputation for price and quality, we expect to prosper in a competitive environment.

5. Negative reactions generally come from customers in other areas of town. They complain that we are not conveniently located. Again, we plan to respond to this complaint by opening additional locations in the future.

6. It is difficult for us to identify small customers. We rely on incentive programs and word of mouth. Presently there are only a few larger customers, all of whom are well known in the industry.

7. Discussed VI C, 1.

8. Substantially lower than expected sales could threaten the success of our expansion. Additional interest expense associated with unsold inventory could significantly increase overhead.

Depending on the degree of difference between projected and actual sales, either we will cut prices to liquidate inventory and suffer the consequences of thinner profit margins, or we will hold excess inventory, absorb the interest charges, and gradually sell surplus at the original price. Our strategy depends on the level of inventories and the type of goods that are not selling as planned.

9. n/a

E. General

1. n/a

VII. CUSTOMERS AND SUPPLIERS

A. Customers

1. We have numerous customers. Since a large portion pay in cash, it is difficult for us to determine sales volume for each. We have approximately four customers who account for more than 5% of our annual sales volume.

2. n/a

3. *

4. Our five largest customers are the largest heating and air conditioning repair firms on the south side. We would have to go outside our geographical territory to come up with prospects of a similar size. Our most promising short term customer prospects are relatively small firms. Complete Supply's management believes that our growth over the next two years will result from increased sales to our existing customer base, which will prosper as the economy recovers. (What's needed: more specific information about how prospective customers are lured to Complete Supply; this answer skirts the issue.)

B. Suppliers

1. *

2. We have several renewable contracts in effect with key suppliers that entitle us to distribute certain product lines exclusively. In return, we must guarantee certain minimum sales levels. We have never had any problem meeting those levels. Since we do a large volume of off-season purchasing, suppliers favor us by shipping back-ordered merchandise to our company before shipping to other distributors.

3. See above, III B, 2. We have exclusive contracts with certain suppliers to carry their items.

VIII. PRODUCTION AND OPERATIONS

A. General

1. Our production process is uncomplicated. Orders are filled from inventory, sorted in stock racks, and delivered to the customers in the front of the store. Inventory levels are tracked on a perpetual basis using an IBM series 3 computer.

2. We replace defective parts on request unless examination of the part reveals that the installation method rather than the part was defective. We return defective parts to the manufacturer for credit. (What's needed: % of parts sold that are defective.)

3. n/a

4. We have the present capacity to double our inventories. (What's needed: more specific information about inventory capacity.)

5. Our building is approximately 30 years old. (What's needed: further description of building.)

6. No injuries.

7. n/a

8. Because we are a large purchaser, our business is solicited regularly by numerous suppliers. This type of competition ensures that we receive the best service and price. We also request quarterly price quotes for high-volume products.

B. Time Constraints

1. Most orders are filled directly out of stock. Back orders are usually filled in an average of 10 days.

2. The only additional cost outlay would be $10,000 for the purchase of additional storage racks.

3. Depending on the supplier and the urgency of the order, our lead time for receiving new stock varies from 3 to 21 days.

4. n/a

5. The most serious delay would occur if forecasted sales levels are not reached. However, we would be able to absorb the additional interest expense associated with excess inventory.

IX. GOVERNMENT REGULATION

A. The company has all the city licenses required to operate its business.

B.–D. n/a

X. FINANCIAL DATA

A. Financial operations

1. *
2. n/a
3. n/a
4. *
5. *
6. *
7. *

8. Because of the many products we sell, and the simplicity of our record-keeping methods, it would be extremely difficult to break down sales by product line or territory.

9. Business is seasonal precisely because it is directly dependent on the weather. Seasonal variations in our heating supply line were offset by the addition of an air conditioning line. Since spring and fall are typically low-volume periods, we tend to offer specials on certain items. We try to push heating and air conditioning items so that more people have an incentive to service their climate control systems during the off months.

10. All inventory is tagged and immediately entered into a computer, which allows us to keep a perpetual inventory cost system. Coupled with our sales forecasts, we can quickly determine what has to be ordered and what our cash needs are. (What's needed: information about how the company tracks cash inflows, other cost data, and gross profit margins.)

11 and **12.** Our most significant costs in the order of importance are:

cost of goods sold

labor (selling expense)

warehousing expense

Cost of goods sold tends to be very stable due to abundant supply and price competition among a large number of manufacturers. Labor supply is very plentiful and therefore not a volatile cost factor. The warehouse monthly mortgage payment is contractually fixed.

13. Our cost position is below that of most of the competition due to our large volume and off-season buying practices. As previously stated, we are also protected from price competition by the convenience and cost savings of our proximity to most of our customers.

B. Financial Condition

1. Insignificant amounts (What's needed: more detail lack of detail implies poor cost control.)
  2. *
  3. n/a
  4. $12,000 for each of the last three years. (What's needed: an explanation of why the company's reserve is so large relative to actual losses over the last three years.)
  5. *
  6. *
  7. *
  8. *
  9. n/a
  10. n/a
  11. n/a
  12. *
  13. *
  14. *
  15. Standard credit procedures:
    a. For continuing customers, past credit history is the only criterion used. If a customer's credit history is clear, we will approve higher credit limits until average payment periods lengthen.
    b. We offer newer customers a minimal credit limit that can be gradually increased based on the customer's payment record. We also offer newer customers who need larger credit approvals an introduction to our banks. (What's needed: more specific description of credit procedures.)
  16. Due to the accuracy of our computerized perpetual inventory system, we have not experienced any significant inventory adjustments over the last three years.
  17. See VIII A, 1.
  18. Slow-moving inventory is not considered obsolete. (What's needed: why isn't slow-moving inventory considered obsolete?)
  19. n/a
  20. *

21. The company owns a 150,000 square foot, single floor, 30-year-old building. Approximately 120,000 square feet are used for inventory stocking while 30,000 square feet are used for office space. There are three truck docks and parking for 100 cars. The building was acquired in 1967 for $2.8 million, against current replacement cost of $3.5 million. Book value is $1.1 million. The structure is in good condition. The building is adjacent to several major highways. Security and rail access are both excellent.

22. Both the company's customer list and location are valuable assets although it would be extremely difficult to place a dollar value on them. Also as previously stated in X, B, 22, the Company's building has an estimated replacement cost of $3.5 million against a book value of $1.1 million.

23. n/a

24. n/a

XI. STRATEGIC PLANNING

A. The company will continue to pursue its off-season purchasing strategy as a means of increasing its market share and profitability. With additional financing, the company will be able to offer an even greater variety of products and thus further increase its market penetration. Eventually, we hope to establish ourselves as the full service supply house that carries even the most difficult to get parts. As our cash flow and market positions strengthen, we will expand into new markets.

B. Inaccurate sales forecasts could substantially increase our inventory financing costs. However, our profit margins are large enough to absorb cost increases. (What's needed: a more thorough risk analysis.)

C. If our growth reaches projected levels, we will open a warehouse on the north side of Chicago. (What's needed: more detail about what levels of growth will allow the company to expand to the north side.)

D. We expect the economy to improve over the next three to five years. Housing starts should increase, as should the resale of old homes. As the housing stock in Chicago continues to grow older, demand for our maintenance and repair products should increase.

E. Although we are moderately affected by economic downturns and depressed construction levels, we can operate profitably with a minimal sales level of replacement and maintenance parts.

Complete Supply Service

a full service heating and air conditioning supplier

3141 S. Morgan Avenue
Chicago, Ill 60608
312-523-0200

October 20, 1982

OVERVIEW

Complete Supply Service sells heating and air conditioning equipment, primarily to small and medium-sized service and contracting firms serving the residential and commercial market in the Chicago area. Many of these firms have been loyal customers for years because they recognize that Complete Supply provides high quality products at low prices. They also remain loyal customers because Complete Supply has an extensive inventory of products on hand.

The company was founded in 1965 by four individuals who had left their previous jobs to gain the independence and the monetary and psychic rewards that operating an independent company can offer. The principals of Complete Supply are Jean Winklereid, Sekhar Bahadur, Charles Bobrinskoy, and Eric Kuby. The company is located on the south side of Chicago. The company owns a 150,000 square foot combination warehouse/office building with quick and easy access to major highways.

Complete Supply's marketing and inventory strategy sets it apart from other suppliers in the Chicago area. The company buys large amounts of inventory in the off season to be resold in peak seasons. Because this practice requires large outlays of cash to purchase inventories, it is somewhat risky. Nonetheless, this strategy has proved more and more profitable as the company's management has become more and more expert at gauging market demand. Traditionally, the sales of heating equipment peak in the winter, and the sales of air conditioning equipment peak in the summer.

The company's practice of purchasing off-season inventory on a profitable basis demands accurate sales forecasting and careful projection of appropriate inventory levels. Complete Supply has repeatedly proven its expertise in this area.

The company's management anticipates a sizable increase in sales of equipment during the next summer season. This sales increase will stem primarily from the recovery of the housing industry in the Chicago area. According to the Department of Commerce, housing starts in the Chicago Standard Metropolitan Statistical Area (SMSA) plummeted in 1982 to an all-time low of less than 10,000 units. The Chicago Chapter of the National Association of Home Builders predicts that housing starts should increase by at least 50% this summer. In addition, the National Association of Realtors projects that the sales of existing homes should nearly double as interest rates continue to level off or even decline, as some optimistic economists predict. This increase in the purchase of existing homes should prove a boon to the company because the buyers of existing homes often desire to upgrade their homes' heating and air conditioning systems.

To continue its successful inventory strategy as the economy recovers, Complete Supply will need to replenish its stock of equipment. However, the company cannot purchase the required inventory from current cash flow and is looking to secure a revolving line of credit of $200,000 from a local bank or finance company. This revolving line of credit will be secured by accounts receivable, inventory, and guarantees from the principals of Complete Supply. The principals are unwilling to give up an equity position to investors.

If the company can secure the requested line of credit for fiscal year 1983, then Complete Supply should be able to increase its year-to-year sales growth rate to an average of 13% during the period 1984 through 1987. This compares to an average year-to-year growth rate of 3% in the years 1978 through 1982. The dramatic increase in sales will be attributable to the higher inventory levels that the company will be able to carry to service its market. According to Market Dynamics, a Chicago-based market research firm, the heating and air conditioning market should grow at a rate of 15% a year. Consequently, Complete Supply's management believes that the company's growth forecast is conservative.

MANAGEMENT

Charles Bobrinskoy, 45, is the president of Complete Supply Service. He holds a bachelor's degree from the Illinois Institute of Technology with a major in mechanical engineering. After graduation he worked as a sales engineer for Heat-Me, a major manufacturer of heating and air conditioning units. During his six-year stint with Heat-Me, Mr. Bobrinskoy acquired a vast knowledge of heating and air conditioning equipment. He grew up in Chicago, the son of a boiler serviceman. His base salary is $60,000, and he receives 5% of the firm's after-tax profits as a profit-sharing bonus. Mr. Bobrinskoy is responsible for day-to-day management of the company; he also approves all inventory purchases.

Jean Winklereid, 47, is vice president and director of operations, and holds a degree in business administration from DePaul University. Ms. Winklereid spent two years working for Arthur Old Accountants, Inc. and then worked six years for Heilman's Furs, where she started as controller and rose to become vice president of finance. She has a base salary of $40,000, plus 5% of the firm's after-tax profits as a profit-sharing bonus. Ms. Winklereid is responsible for negotiating with suppliers, establishing inventory levels, and forecasting projected sales.

Sekhar Bahadur, 46, is vice president and chief financial officer. He holds a degree in finance from Northern Illinois University. Mr. Bahadur worked previously as CFO for Salosachs, a local real estate investment firm. Mr. Bahadur is responsible for structuring financing, preparing budgets, evaluating investments, and compiling the company's financial statements. He also monitors the company's inventory control system. Mr. Bahadur earns a base salary of $40,000 plus 5% of the firm's after-tax profits.

Eric Kuby, 44, is vice president and director of marketing. Mr. Kuby holds a degree in business administration from Loyola University. Mr. Kuby spent 15 years working for the Jewel Food Stores, starting as assistant store manager, advancing to store manager, and then to assistant director of marketing. Mr. Kuby's responsibilities include setting advertising budgets, devising advertising and promotion strategies, and developing and increasing the company's customer base. Mr. Kuby earns a base salary of $40,000 plus 5% of the firm's after-tax profits.

STRENGTHS AND WEAKNESSES OF MANAGEMENT

All the officers of the company are talented persons with extensive experience in their respective fields. Each individual has particular strengths that complement the strengths of the other three. Management has the skills in the four major areas—engineering, operations, finance, and marketing—that are essential in running a heating and air conditioning supply service. Each member of management has made a major commitment to the business. They have worked together for over 15 years and have developed a rapport that has helped the business to remain profitable despite difficult economic times. The management of Complete Supply Service devotes 100% of its working time to the affairs of the company. Consequently, these individuals have no conflicts of interest.

The major weakness of the company's management structure is the division of labor. Although Mr. Bobrinskoy has a vast knowledge of products and technology, he has less knowledge than Mr. Kuby does about marketing. If Mr. Bobrinskoy were to leave the company—an unlikely prospect—there would be a tremendous gap in management structure. However, since each member of management has been in the business at least 15 years, each individual has acquired a fundamental knowledge of the other aspects of the business. Even if a member of management were to leave the business, the remaining principals could keep the business running until a suitable replacement could be found.

However, it is extremely unlikely that any member of the management team would join a competitor or leave to start a new business. Even though the principals have not signed covenants not to compete, the four principals have devoted such an extensive portion of their careers and have such a substantial stake in the business that leaving Complete Supply is virtually out of the question.

Complete Supply is currently training several individuals in each of the divisions to take over management of the existing operation ultimately, thus allowing the partners to focus on long-range goals. Management trainees are taught by the apprenticeship program and already given a large degree of freedom to make decisions. All are performing exceedingly well.

The only management team members who might defect would be the trainees. Upon completion of the apprenticeship program, however, they will receive larger salaries and bonuses that will be tied to their performance. They will receive total compensation that far exceeds what they would expect to earn for similar employement.

GOALS OF MANAGEMENT

Management wants to continue operating a profitable company, and increase market share within the Chicago area. All officers wish to continue private ownership of the firm.

REFERENCES AND COUNSEL

The following references are available to comment on the capabilities of the management of Complete Supply Service. These organizations have also provided counsel in their various fields of specialty. They are all located in Chicago.

Viola, Ross and Associates, accountants. Contact Mr. John Ross, managing partner. He oversees the company's yearly audit. 312-555-1243.

Steinman, Markowitz, Brown, Brown and Brown, lawyers. Contact Mr. Rudolph Brown, senior partner. He oversees all the legal affairs of the company. 312-555-1826.

Exchange National Bank, Mr. David Rudes, vice president, small business lending. He is the bank's contact with the company. 312-555-0985.

American National Bank. Ms. Mary Rudes, executive vice president. She is the bank's contact with the company. 312-555-4173.

First National Bank. Mr. Clay Rose, senior vice president. He is the bank's contact with the company. 312-555-4860.

First City Management Consultants. Mr. Michael Jurkash, vice president. Mr. Jurkash has provided management consulting services to the company, particularly in the area of inventory control. 312-555-4910.

Mount McKinsey and Associate Management Consultants. Ms. Rose Lyon, vice president. Ms. Lyon has provided management consulting services, particularly in the area of marketing strategy. 312-555-0141.

All of the above are business acquaintances. A list of major customers and suppliers is included in the section entitled Customers and Suppliers.

OWNERSHIP

The company's stock, which is equally divided among the four principals (see Management), bears a legend stating that it cannot be freely traded without complying with certain securities' laws and regulations. The principals also have right of first refusal—i.e., any principal who wants to sell his stock to a third party must first offer his stock to the other principals. The company does not currently make available either stock options or stock bonuses to any of its employees. The company has taken out life insurance on each of the principals; these policies are provided by Stalwart Insurance Co., Newport, RI. In the event of a principal's death, this insurance will provide funds allowing the company to purchase the stock of the deceased principal. Of the 10,000 shares of common stock authorized, 1000 have been issued, 250 shares to each principal.

PRODUCTS

Complete Supply Service originally sold only heating supplies. These supplies varied at first from medium to lower priced items. Typically they were safety controls for boilers, air ducts, pipe, motors, fans, pumps, thermostats, and thermocouples. This product line was designed to supply a serviceperson with any small- or medium-sized part he/she might need to make repairs or upgrade a unit. Often, a serviceperson will make a service call without knowing exactly what the problem is. Upon inspection of the customer's heating unit, he/she might isolate the difficulty in a defective part. Not having the part on hand, he/she would purchase the product from us. We later added air conditioning products with the same philosophy in mind.

As we grew, we were able to cut our prices on both heating and air conditioning lines by purchasing such goods in the off season. With the additional profits, we then began stocking major heating and air conditioning items for installers and contractors. These items included boilers and air conditioners for installation in new structures and for retrofits. The company does not stock very large commercial heating and air conditioning units precisely because those firms that install such units are able to purchase direct from the factories and because such very large items tend to turnover very slowly.

Complete Supply enjoys a superior market position in the supply business. According to research done by the Chicago firm Dynamic Market Analysis, the company currently has nearly a 60% market share of the south side supply business. Companies wishing to enter the market would have a difficult time competing simply because Complete Supply enjoys a solid reputation, substantial financial resources, a large inventory, and knowledgeable support staff. In the larger Chicago-area market, we are able to compete with other supply houses because of our low prices and extensive inventory. Servicepeople who service other areas of the city often stock up their inventories when they are purchasing from us. Complete Supply's dominance in the local market enables us to purchase from major manufacturers at a discount even during peak season. We are thus able to offer our customers attractive credit terms that emerging supply houses cannot afford to match. This is extremely helpful to servicepeople who experience a lag between the time they purchase parts from us and the time they collect funds from their customer.

Inventory obsolescence is low. Boilers have a relatively long life. Ductwork and piping rarely if ever become obsolete. Unlike automobiles, heating and air conditioning parts do not become obsolete because of style. Any inventory that might become obsolete rather rapidly, i.e., computerized thermostats, are purchased with the right of return to the manufacturers. The same holds true for the latest line of energy-efficient furnaces. Many servicepeople and contractors would rather install a part they are familiar with than a technologically more advanced new part, even if the new part is superior and would render the old part obsolete.

INSURANCE

All of our officers are insured with key-man insurance from Specialized Management Insurance Corporation, Akron, Ohio. The company would receive compensation for lost expertise. The buildings and inventories are fully covered by a variable policy from the Policeman's Fund Insurance Company, Tulsa, Okla. This policy scales payments according to level of inventory. The company pays a premium for such a policy— 10% over the industry average. However, when one considers the potential loss of even a small portion of the company's potential inventory, the principals feel such a premium is earned (see also Ownership).

LOCATION

The company's warehouse and offices are located close to Chicago's four major highways—Interstates 94, 294, 81, and 64. Most of the firm's initial customers bought from Complete Supply because of the company's proximity to their work site. Although the south side location is competively dominant in its own sphere of influence, the company loses potential business from the north side to local north side supply houses. However, if the $200,000 loan is arranged, the company should be profitable enough to expand the business to the north side by acquiring or leasing additional warehouse space. Being located in Chicago is a benefit since we are able to draw on a large pool of labor.

LEGAL

Complete Supply Service is an Illinois Corporation. No lawsuits have been filed against the company, and none is likely to be filed in the near future. Since almost all the products Complete Supply sells have manufacturer's warranties, the company is minimally liable for their defects. The company has all the business licenses required to operate a business in the city of Chicago.

EMPLOYEES

Below is a table that shows how many employees the company has had in the past three years, and how many the company plans to have in the next three years.

Number of Employees			
Fiscal Year	1979	1980	1981
Full-time	15	17	22
Part-time	2	4	6
Fiscal Year	1982	1983	1984
Full-time	22	25	27
Part-time	8	8	8

Roughly 50% of the full-time employees can be considered skilled workers. These include forklift operators and customer service representatives. Employee costs are approximately 15% of sales. All of the part-time help is unskilled. The company's workers have no union affiliations.

Because of the abundant labor pool of both skilled and unskilled workers, the company has no problem hiring new workers or replacing unsatisfactory ones. This is true for both full- and part-time workers.

All employees are entitled to paid vacations depending on number of years worked. Each employee receives one week paid vacation for every two years worked until an employee has reached ten years service. Employees have a maximum of five vacation weeks per year. Each employee receives one week of unpaid vacation per year. The company also offers a small optional health medical plan.

Salaries for skilled and unskilled workers are competitive. According to *Heating and Air Conditioning Retailer* magazine, the average salary for skilled employees in supply firms like Complete Supply is $14.00 per hour. We offer an average of $16.00 per hour. For unskilled workers, the magazine quotes an average hourly wage of $6.00. We offer an average of $8.00 per hour.

The company does require skilled employees to work the order desk. They answer questions that customers have and identify parts that a customer needs. Most of these employees were former service-people who left the field for various reasons. We have had no problem hiring employees with the required level of experience.

Management enjoys a productive working relationship with the company's employees. As fair employers, the company has ensured that employees are paid competitively and hard-working employees are justly rewarded. The company has experienced no work stoppages.

Our sales force can be adjusted to sales volume, but we do not do so. In periods of low volume, we shorten the employees' work hours, schedule employees to take vacation, and perform inventory checks and maintenance work. Even though seasonal fluctuations might make it advantageous to scale down the company's labor force, the management believes that maintaining the staff through leaner times cultivates loyal and motivated employees.

The company's unskilled labor turnover is relatively high compared to our skilled turnover. Unskilled labor usually performs manual labor tasks such as filling stock and orders. Average employment is roughly 2.5 years. Skilled labor turnover is lower. The company loses about one person per four years.

Because management feels they are unnecessary, the company does not have training programs for unskilled workers. A new worker is simply paired with a seasoned worker for a few days. As for skilled workers, most of these people have extensive experience and need only to learn the company's paperwork procedures.

INVESTMENT CRITERIA

Complete Supply is seeking a $200,000 revolving line of credit to finance the purchase of additional inventories. The principals of the company prefer not to give up any equity. Internally generated cash flow should be sufficient to cover principal and interest on the credit line requested. A second lien on current accounts receivable and inventory will be offered along with a second mortgage on the company's building as collateral. Also, the principals are willing to provide personal guarantees of $50,000 each. (Each principal has a net worth of over $100,000).

The company currently enjoys banking relationships with the three banks listed in REFERENCES AND COUNSEL; those banks will be approached for the requested loan. The company currently has a revolving line of credit with Exchange National Bank totaling $200,000 at terms of 2.5% above prime floating. The company is required by the bank to repay its loan completely for a period of thirty days during each year. This line of credit is secured by a first lien on inventory and accounts receivable. Bank borrowing are used to cover normal purchases of inventory but are inadequate to cover forecasted purchases connected with a substantial growth in volume. All payments are current.

The company will draw down $50,000 of the requested revolving credit line in each of the four quarters of 1983.

COMPETITION

The company enjoys a local dominance in the 20 square mile area contiguous to our location where Complete Supply has a 60% share of market, according to research done by Market Dynamics. However, in the Chicago area, which encompasses approximately 900 square miles, Complete Supply is roughly fifth.

Below is a list of the company's major competitors and management's best estimate of their sales volume.

STRENGTHS AND WEAKNESSES OF COMPETITION

Because all of Complete Supply's competitors are privately held, the evaluation of their strengths and weaknesses is derived from management's best estimates of their financial positions.

Bob Mason is the only other firm that is probably better capitalized than Complete Supply Service. Most of the sales generated by the other firms result from their convenient location to local customers. While other, smaller supply houses compete in their own neighborhoods, none of them is able to underprice major houses that obtain price dis-

	Market Share
Bob Mason & Co. 125th and Stewart (southwest side) Est. Sales of $4.5 million privately held firm	11.25%
Harvey Supply 5164 W. Daley (west side) Est. Sales of $4 million privately held firm	10%
Rosenbaum Heating Supply 2436 N. River (north side) Est. Sales of $4.25 million privately held firm	10.6%
George Gerson and Company 3200 West Main (northwest side) Estimated Sales of $3.75 million privately held	9.3%
Gregorious' Sales 5300 North Stewart (north side) Est. Sales of $3.5 million privately held	8.75%

counts for volume purchases. Gregorious has established a reputation for service by offering on-the-job delivery service for even small purchase items.

None of the above firms has purchased off season as aggressively as has Complete Supply. Most of the competition's officers lack Complete Supply's buying expertise. Competitors are also prevented from carrying certain lines due to Complete Supply's exclusive relationship with manufacturers.

Complete Supply's plans for increasing market share and expanding beyond the south side could be thwarted if one of the company's major competitors began purchasing off season as aggressively as Complete Supply does. However, only the well-capitalized Mason is in a position to do so; it is the only Chicago-area supply firm that has the warehouse space required to stock off-season inventory.

Fortunately, Complete Supply's management believes Mason lacks the financial and management expertise to implement this strategy. Even if Mason had the resources to emulate Complete Supply's strategy, the company would continue to benefit from its local monopoly. The other houses rely on high inventory turnover.

Competition would intensify if other supply firms in the Chicago area served by Complete Supply were to build additional warehouse capacity in order to take advantage of off-season purchasing. Complete Supply plans to protect itself from this possibility by establishing the company on the north side of the city as quickly as possible. With Complete Supply's established name and reputation for low price and high quality, management expects the company to prosper in a highly competitive environment.

MARKETING STRATEGY

The total market for heating and air conditioning equipment in the Chicago area is roughly $40 million dollars, although next year the market should increase to roughly $45 million and by 1988 to $65 million, according to Market Dynamics. A large number of gas boilers were installed in the early 1970s after passage of EPA laws made coal-burning heaters impractical. Complete Supply forecasts that most of these heaters will be experiencing breakdowns, causing increased demand for parts and new units. The increasing success of heat pumps and efficient air conditioners should also help the market reach $65 million.

Due to the need for the replacement of defective parts, Complete Supply enjoys a relatively assured demand for its products. During periods of prosperity, people tend to install boilers while in leaner times they purchase parts to repair them. Consumers, faced with the escalating cost of deregulated natural gas, should be a strong market for replacement parts to maintain their units at the highest level of efficiency.

Below are the five reasons why customers purchase from Complete Supply.

1. Proximity
2. Low price for high quality parts
3. Support staff (behind the counter order takers)
4. Credit terms for good customers
5. Large inventory, ensuring good order fill

But perhaps the most important reason that customers rely on Complete Supply is that they need to purchase a part at a low price from a supplier that will most likely have the part in stock. Complete Supply's customers are profit oriented. They want to spend most of their time on a job where they can charge for their services. They want quality parts so they won't have to return to replace a new part that is defective. They can get those quality parts at Complete Supply.

Complete Supply's management is in constant contact with its customers; consequently, the company can adjust to the customer's needs. Management trains order-fillers to monitor the desires of the company's customers. If they are unhappy with a product, or if they would like Complete Supply to provide a product the company does not have in stock, Complete Supply will consider appropriate changes.

The company's management anticipates that more and more independent servicepeople will be absorbed by larger companies. Thus, Complete Supply is attempting to attract large customers through a telemarketing effort led by Ms. Winklereid. Also, the reputation the company has established with smaller servicepeople, many of whom will be absorbed by larger customers, should help Complete Supply attract those larger firms. The company will market to the large customer the way it markets to the serviceperson; low pricing, quality product, quick and efficient order filling, solid support staff and good credit terms.

Marketing Methods

Complete Supply's most effective marketing tool is word of mouth. Servicemen and general contractors are a hard market to hit. Consequently, Complete Supply takes a diversified approach to marketing strategy. At local trade shows, Complete Supply will rent prime booth space. Also, the company's management is active in a number of local chapters of trade organizations such as the American Society for Heating, Refrigeration and Air Conditioning (ASHRAC), the Association of General Contractors, and others. Complete Supply's management maintains a mailing list of previous customers. Twice a year (April 1 and November 1) Complete Supply sends out a flyer promoting the company's extensive stock of inventory. The company also offers incentives for previous customers to bring in new customers; this incentive ranges from a 5% to a 10% discount. Complete Supply also has a one-fourth page Yellow Pages advertisement, and on occasion Complete Supply will advertise in the geographical editions of trade publications such as *ASHRAC Journal* and *Heating Piping and Air Conditioning*. However, trade journal advertising has yet to prove an adequately effective marketing tool since even a geographical edition has too wide an audience for Complete Supply. Trade journal advertising will be evaluated more closely if the company expands to serve the entire Chicago area.

It is hard to identify small service companies, so Complete Supply relies on word of mouth and incentive programs outlined above. Mr. Kuby conducts an ongoing telemarketing effort to contact potential small customers; the names of these potential customers are acquired primarily through association membership lists and Yellow Page listings.

Complete Supply has achieved an excellent reputation with its customers. However, many potential customers beyond Complete Supply's immediate geographical react negatively to the company's marketing efforts: they say the company is too far away. Management plans to alleviate this problem by opening a north side warehouse.

Potential Marketing Problems and Their Solutions

Complete Supply's marketing strategy hinges on being able to purchase aggressively large amounts of inventory. If projected sales are overly optimistic, the company has plenty of warehouse space to house the inventory. Thus, management's major concern would be the additional interest charges associated with unsold inventory. If sales do not reach expected levels, management has two options. It can either cut prices to liquidate the inventory to a reasonable level and suffer from slimmer profit margins, or it can hold the inventory and pay the interest charges.

The first option—slashing prices to eliminate inventory—would be chosen if sales fall far short of expectations. This option would also be selectively applied to the excess inventory of big ticket items such as larger heating and air conditioning units. The second option will be chosen if sales fall slightly short of expectations. Then the revenues from the eventual sale of the remaining product lines should be sufficient to cover additional interest charges, in addition to providing a reasonable profit.

CUSTOMERS AND SUPPLIERS

Complete Supply has many customers. Since many customers are one-time users of Complete Supply and pay in cash, estimates of the number of customers would be very rough approximations. The company has five customers who together account for more than 10% of our annual sales volume. They are listed below. Credit rating ranges from 1 to 10, with 10 the best.

Robert Climate Control 240 S. McMillan Chicago, Ill	Customer since 1974 Credit rating 10
Wagner Heating 3571 Broadway Chicago, Ill	Customer since 1975 Credit rating 9
Manley Heating 4302 S. Waukegan Chicago, Ill	Customer since 1978 Credit rating 8.5
Krause Koolers 6036 S. Boulevard Chicago, Ill	Customer since 1972 Credit rating 10
Jones Control 1203 E. 46th St. Chicago, Ill	Customer since 1978 Credit rating 9

These firms are, in management's best estimate, the largest heating and air conditioning installation and repair firms on the city's south side.

Below is a list of Complete Supply Service's top five customers and the amount and the percentage of sales each accounts for.

PERCENT OF SALES—FIVE TOP CUSTOMERS

			($000)			
	1980	1981	1982	1983	1984	1985
Total sales	2987	3268	3302	3665	4105	4638
Robert	119	130	132	145	164	185
	4%	4%	4%	4%	4%	4%
Wagner	89	98	99	109	123	139
	3%	3%	3%	3%	3%	3%
Manley	59.5	65	66	73	82	93
	2%	2%	2%	2%	2%	2%
Krause	29	33	33	36	41	46
	1%	1%	1%	1%	1%	1%
Jones	14.9	16	17	18	20	23
	.5%	.5%	.5%	.5%	.5%	.5%

Prospective Customers

Complete Supply makes contact with prospective customers through the company's current clientele. They are usually the best source of information about prospective customers. As a rule, potential customers seek out Complete Supply because of our low prices and extensive inventory. Complete Supply also offers a special "set-up" inventory package, designed specifically for the starting serviceperson or contractor. This set up is offered at a large discount.

Suppliers

Below are Complete Supply's major suppliers, the volume purchased from them, and the extent of the company's credit line.

MAJOR SUPPLIERS TO COMPLETE SUPPLY

	vol. purchase ($000)	max. credit
South Control 123 E. 25th St. Central, Mo.	46.6	20
McCaffry Controls 5936 W. Main Waukegan, Ill	39	20
Krakow Boilers and Burners 4306 Elizabeth Lane Pittston, NJ	34.3	20
Martin Supply 1306 Lake Champaign, Ill	23.4	15
Peter GTX Corp. 8434 Myrlte Lexington, Ky.	15.6	10

Complete Supply has contracts that give the company exclusive distributorship rights for several product lines. In return, Complete Supply must guarantee certain minimum sales levels. Meeting these levels has never been a problem. Because of Complete Supply's high volume and off-season buying practices, suppliers favor the company by ship-ping back-ordered merchandise to our company before shipping to other distributors.

Because Complete Supply is a large purchaser, the company is so-licited regularly by numerous suppliers. This type of competition en-sures that we receive the best service and price. Management also re-quests quarterly price quotes for high-volume products.

PRODUCTION AND OPERATIONS

Complete Supply's production process is uncomplicated. Orders are filled from inventory, sorted in stock racks, and delivered to the cus-tomer at the front of the store. As orders are taken and the product sold, inventory data are automatically entered into the company's computer through electronic cash registers. The computer perpetually tracks all inventory.

Complete Supply will replace any defective part unless it has been installed improperly. Complete Supply then receives credit for such defective parts from the manufacturer. (Because of Complete Supply's size, the company is usually able to deal directly with manufacturers and avoid purchasing from distributors.) Less than 2% of the compa-ny's inventory is returned as defective to the manufacturers.

The inventory capacity of Complete Supply depends on the particu-lar product and its price. Complete Supply currently carries nearly one thousand separate product items ranging from pipe fittings to 25,000 BTU air conditioners. Naturally, the company will likely carry more units of lower priced items than higher priced items.

Over the past three years, Complete Supply has carried an average of 60% of its inventory capacity, due to the general economic slump. Now the company has the capacity to double inventories. Our one-story, brick building is approximately 30 years old, but it is in excellent condition. Five years ago the company installed new inventory racks. If the company acquires the requested financing, $10,000 would be spent on new storage racks.

Complete Supply's inventory turnover is low (See ratio analysis at end.) This allows the company to provide fast service for customers. Depending on the supplier and the urgency of the order, the lead time for receiving new stock varies from 3 to 21 days. (Back orders are filled in an average of ten days.)

The company's personnel have experienced no major on-the-job injuries.

FINANCIAL

At the end of this business plan, the investor will find the necessary financial statements to judge adequately the performance and prospects of Complete Supply. Among those statements are a breakeven analysis, projected income statement, and cash flow analyses. The following section discusses the unique aspects of Complete Supply and how they affect the company's financial position.

Seasonality

Because Complete Supply sells heating and air conditioning supplies, its business is highly seasonal. The company has yet to experience the major ill effect of carrying seasonal lines, namely, substantial inventory carrying costs if inventory is not sold. The variations in the company's cash flow are not as great as one might think. Since spring and fall are typically low-volume periods, the company promotes the sale of air conditioner and boiler care items during these off months. But even then, these low-volume periods are not a drain on the company's resources since many people install boilers and air conditioners during periods of favorable weather. Also the two different lines tend to offset each other so that air conditioning product sales increase as heating product sales decline, and vice versa.

Costs and Cash Flow Control Systems

All the company's inventory is tagged and the stock number is immediately entered into the computer, allowing the company's management to keep a watchful eye on inventory. Management is highly experienced in gauging projected sales and stocking inventory to meet those projections. When an item is sold, data is simultaneously entered into a computer through electronic cash registers. If the customer does not pay cash, an invoice is mailed within seven days requesting payment within 30 days unless special arrangements have been made.

Management does not consider most slow-moving obsolete because the heating and air conditioning industry has not experienced major technological advances. Because of this industry characteristic, most products have a lengthy shelf life. Even if certain products are supplanted by more advanced models, the older versions can often be used to replace existing models that require repair.

Intangible Assets

Both the company's customer list and locations are valuable assets, although it would be extremely difficult to place a dollar value on them (see Real Property for a conservative estimate of the building's value).

Fixed and Variable Costs

For Complete Supply, the highest cost is naturally the cost of goods sold. The cost of labor (selling expense) and warehousing expense rank next as significant costs for the company. Because most products, with some exceptions, are basically similar regardless of manufacturer, most of the merchandise that Complete Supply carries is competitively priced. And, of course, Complete Supply's aggressive off-season buying keeps the cost of goods down. Even if prices should fluctuate or increase dramatically—an unlikely prospect—Complete Supply will have an adequate inventory to withstand such volatility. Labor costs are not volatile due to a large labor pool and a relatively low skill requirement. Both depreciation and interest expense are "locked in" according to predetermined schedules.

Price Pressures

Because Complete Supply purchases so aggressively in the off season, the company is able to pass on the lowest cost basis in the industry to customers in the form of lower prices. Thus it's highly unlikely that the company's competitors would engage in a price war to lure customers. Since most of the company's customers work nearby, competitors would have to undercut Complete Supply's prices substantially to make it worthwhile for the customer to travel the 45 minutes on average it would take to reach a competitive outlet.

Should industry demand suddenly collapse—a doubtful prospect given the cold Chicago winters and the perpetual need for heating equipment and spare parts—Complete Supply would return a substantial portion of its inventory to manufacturers.

Status of Accounts Receivable

Complete Supply has a handful of accounts that are uncollectible and have been recently written off. The amount totals less than $1000.

Below is a list of the company's accounts receivable that are more than 90 days old.

Account	amount	days old
Greenfield	$ 7,000	95
Marks	$ 8,900	150
Smith	$14,000	95
Taylor	$12,000	95
Watson	$ 6,500	120
Robbin's	$ 9,200	95

All of these customers have been reliable in the past and, until the recent recession, have kept their accounts current. Complete Supply has obtained financial statements from delinquent customers to determine the collectability of each account. Management believes these delinquent accounts will be collectible. The company reserved $12,000 for each of the past three fiscal years for bad debts. Write-offs have been $2500, $3400, and $1200 over each of the last three years. Although the company's historical write-off level previously justified the $12,000 reserve, improved credit practices have substantially reduced actual write-offs.

Credit Procedures

Complete Supply has two basic credit procedures:

1. For continuing customers, past credit history and Dun & Bradstreet reports are the only two guidelines used. If the customer's payment history is good, we will increase his credit until payments exceed 45 days. At that point, the customer's credit line is frozen until he brings his account current.
2. The company allows new customers to build up credit gradually. After checking with the customer's bank, and three additional references, we will grant the customer up to a $5000 open line. New customers also have the option of securing a bank loan if they require a larger amount of trade credit. We will introduce customers to our banks as an additional courtesy.

Real Property

Complete Supply owns a 150,000 square foot warehouse which it acquired in mid-1967 for $2.8 million. Approximately 120,000 square feet are used to stock inventory. The balance is used for offices and other administrative purposes. The building has three truck docks to load and unload material. The structure is one-story brick and kept up to code. Current replacement cost is around $3.5 million, according to Best Appraisers, a Chicago-based appraisal firm (appraisal was completed February, 1982). Book value is $1.1 million. The structure is 30 years old.

STRATEGIC PLAN AND RISKS

Complete Supply wants to continue its aggressive policy of buying large quantities of heating and air conditioning supply inventory. With the economy poised for recovery and interest rates falling, the company's management believes this is the opportune moment to get an edge on the competition. Complete Supply wants to establish its reputation as the supply house to rely on for even the most difficult to get parts. Increasing inventory dramatically will help the company establish that reputation. Management also wants Complete Supply to acquire the reputation as a supply house that carries parts no one else has; the company's increasing inventory capacity will help encourage manufacturers to sign exclusive area retail sales contracts with Complete Supply.

After Complete Supply's cash position and reputation have been strengthened, management would like to open an additional outlet on the north side of the city. At first, this warehouse should be moderately-sized, 15,000 to 20,000 square feet, and the company should lease rather than buy. This smaller warehouse will allow Complete Supply to get a foothold on the north side market without placing undue strain on the company's resources. If this new warehouse turns a profit within a year, Complete Supply's management will consider increasing warehouse space, provided the general economic situation proves favorable. It should, however, be noted that the requested loan would only be used for inventory expansion, rather than for the expansion to the north side.

The north side is clearly the next growth market for the heating and air conditioning supply business. According to the local chapter of the National Association of Realtors, nearly two-thirds of the housing starts in the next three years will occur in the northwest quadrant of the Chicago SMSA.

The National Association of Realtors has also said that 75% of the condominium conversions inside the Chicago city limits will occur north of Division Street. Although condominium conversions have slowed in the past two years, declining interest rates will make condominium purchases more attractive, thus stimulating conversions. The city of Chicago has also authorized a subsidized low interest rate mortgage program and a pool of funds for home improvement, both of which should allow consumers to purchase and upgrade their homes. Increasing conversions will mean more business for equipment suppliers because renovators will want to repair and/or replace heating and air conditioning units.

But even if housing starts remain sluggish, and even if home resales and condominium conversions do not reach expected levels, the market for heating and air conditioning supplies should remain healthy.

The reason for this is straightforward: the Chicago SMSA housing stock is growing old. According to the local office of the Department of Commerce, the average house in the Chicago SMSA is nearly 35 years old. This aging housing stock requires continual upkeep and repair. Although it is impossible to pinpoint precisely how much of that housing stock will need new heating and air conditioning systems in the next three to five years, Complete Supply's customers (servicemen and contractors) constantly refer to the deteriorating condition of the facilities they service. To maintain acceptable living conditions, the users of these facilities will have to upgrade them.

Risks

Like every business, Complete Supply is affected by the general economic situation. If interest rates should increase above 13%, then the housing recovery would be crushed, thus curtailing Complete Supply's opportunity to supply that growing market. Such an interest rate increase would also dampen the incentive to undertake condominium conversions and heating/air conditioning plant repairs in general. If the economy would take a turn for the worse, and Complete Supply had acquired its additional inventory, then the company would clearly be in a breakeven financial position. However, management believes that the economy will rebound.

Even if the economy takes a turn for the worse, however, Complete Supply would be able to carry additional inventory without risking any permanent damage to the business. The management is skilled at weathering difficult times. During the recession of 1980–1982, the company turned an acceptable profit, despite the depressed markets.

Management is confident that it could liquidate inventory in an orderly fashion so that any additional debt could be serviced without difficulty.

FINANCIAL PROFILE

Assumptions Behind Financial Statements

These statements assume that Complete Supply will acquire a new revolving line of credit of $200,000 in 1983, in addition to an existing $200,000 line of credit for total bank loan availability of $400,000. Interest payments on both lines of credit are calculated at 16% (prime plus 2½% floating) in the years 1983 through 1987. Annual borrowings are expected to average $350,000. As has been the practice in the past, it is assumed that both lenders will request that the company completely repay its loans during the year for a period of thirty days. Accordingly, the year-end balance sheet does *not* reflect usage under either revolving line of credit. The interest rate of 16% is predicated on the assumption that prime interest will average 13.5% during the period 1983-1987. Management believes that 16% is a conservative interest figure.

These statements also assume a conservative compounded annual growth rate in sales through the years 1983-1987 of 13.7%, a growth rate below the 15% projected by Market Dynamics.

The company's building and associated equipment were acquired in mid-1967 for $2.825 million and are being depreciated over a 25-year life on a straight line basis.

The current mortgage on the company's building was renegotiated in mid-1970 for a total principal value of $2.26 million. Principal payments of $113,000 are required annually for a period of 20 years ending in mid-1990. Interest is calculated at 5% of the outstanding balance.

The company's dividend policy is arbitrary rather than tied to a percentage of earnings or cash flow.

Income taxes are calculated at 42% of pretax income.

Assumptions Behind Breakeven Analysis

1. This analysis assumes the total Chicago area market is $40 million in 1983, $45 million in 1984, $55 million in 1985, $60 million in 1986, and $65 million in 1987.
2. Variable costs are assumed to be 75% of sales. Fixed costs are assumed to be 30% of selling expenses plus interest expense. These percentages are based on past experience.
3. Breakeven points were calculated using the following equation:

$$\text{Breakeven Sales} = \frac{(\text{Actual Revenues})(\text{Fixed Costs})}{(\text{Actual Revenues} - \text{Variable Costs})}$$

4. The company's warehouse has a total capacity of $5 million.

COMPLETE SUPPLY: FINANCIAL STATEMENTS

Balance Sheet in Thousands	Actual			Projected				
	1980	1981	1982	1983	1984	1985	1986	1987
Current Assets								
Cash	3.24	3.27	3.30	3.30	3.30	3.30	3.30	3.30
Receivables	30.12	30.43	30.73	34.11	38.21	43.18	49.65	57.10
Inventories	248.95	251.46	254.00	281.94	315.77	356.82	410.35	471.90
Current Assets Total	282.30	285.16	288.04	319.36	357.28	403.30	463.30	532.30
Property, plant and equipment	1319.00	1206.00	1093.00	980.00	867.00	754.00	641.00	528.00
Total Assets	1601.30	1491.16	1381.04	1299.36	1224.28	1157.30	1104.30	1060.30
Liabilities and Equity								
Accounts Payable	32.36	32.69	33.02	36.65	41.05	46.39	53.35	61.35
Mortgage Payable	1104.00	991.00	878.00	765.00	652.00	539.00	426.00	313.00
Common Stock	40.00	40.00	40.00	40.00	40.00	40.00	40.00	40.00
Retained Earnings	424.94	427.47	430.02	457.70	491.23	531.91	584.96	645.95
Total Liabilities and Equity	1601.30	1491.16	1381.04	1299.36	1224.28	1157.30	1104.30	1060.30

COMPLETE SUPPLY: FINANCIAL STATEMENTS

Income Statement in Thousands	Actual				Projected			
	1980	1981	1982	1983	1984	1985	1986	1987
Sales of Merchandise	2987.34	3268.98	3302.00	3665.22	4105.05	4638.70	5334.51	6134.68
Expenses								
Cost of goods sold	2240.51	2451.74	2476.50	2748.92	3078.78	3479.03	4000.88	4601.01
Selling Expense	537.72	588.42	594.36	659.74	738.91	834.97	960.21	1104.24
Depreciation	113.00	113.00	113.00	113.00	113.00	113.00	113.00	113.00
Operating margin	96.11	115.83	118.14	143.57	174.35	211.71	260.42	316.43
Interest on Mortgage	55.20	49.55	43.90	38.25	32.60	26.95	21.30	15.65
Interest on Revolving Credit	34.00	32.00	28.00	56.00	56.00	56.00	56.00	56.00
Earnings before Taxes	6.91	34.28	46.24	49.32	85.75	128.76	183.12	244.78
Income Tax	2.90	14.40	19.42	20.71	36.02	54.08	76.91	102.81
Net Income	4.01	19.88	26.82	28.60	49.74	74.68	106.21	141.97
Dividends	1.51	17.36	24.27	.91	16.21	34.00	53.17	80.97
Cash Flow (Net Income & Depreciation)	117.01	132.88	139.82	141.60	162.74	187.68	219.21	254.97

Variances in balancing figures are attributable to rounding error.

COMPLETE SUPPLY: FINANCIAL STATEMENTS

Sources and Uses of Working Capital (in thousands)	Actual			Projected		
	1980	1981	1982	1983	1984	1985
Sources of Funds						
Net Income	4.01	19.88	26.82	28.60	49.74	74.68
Depreciation	113.00	113.00	113.00	113.00	113.00	113.00
Net from Operations	117.01	132.88	139.82	141.60	162.74	187.68
Uses of Funds						
Mortgage Principal Repayment	113.00	113.00	113.00	113.00	113.00	113.00
Dividends	1.51	17.36	24.27	0.91	16.21	34.00
Net Use of Funds	114.51	130.36	137.27	113.91	129.21	147.00
Net Increase (Decrease) In Working Capital	2.50	2.52	2.55	27.69	33.53	40.68
Changes in Components of Working Capital						
Cash	0.04	0.03	0.03	—	—	—
Accounts Receivable	0.30	0.31	0.30	3.38	4.10	4.97
Inventory	2.49	2.51	2.54	27.94	33.83	41.05
Total Current Assets	2.83	2.85	2.87	31.32	37.93	46.02
Accounts Payable	0.32	0.33	0.33	3.63	4.40	5.34
Total Current Liabilities	0.32	0.33	0.33	3.63	4.40	5.34
Net Increase (Decrease) in Working Capital	*2.51	2.52	*2.54	27.69	33.53	40.68

*Variances in balancing figures are attributable to rounding error.

COMPLETE SUPPLY

Projected Breakeven Analysis (in thousands)	Cash Flow Analysis				
	1983	1984	1985	1986	1987
30% of Selling Expenses	198	222	250	288	331
Interest Expense	94.3	88.6	83.0	77.3	71.7
Total Fixed Costs	292.3	310.6	333.0	365.3	402.7
Breakeven Sales Volume	1169.2	1242.4	1332.0	1461.2	1610.8
Market Share Required	2.9%	2.8%	2.4%	2.4%	2.5%
Capacity Utilization	23.0%	25.0%	27.0%	29.0%	32.0%
	Net Income Analysis				
Fixed Costs Plus Depreciation	405.3	423.6	446.0	478.3	515.7
Breakeven Sales Volume	1621.2	1694.4	1784.0	1913.2	2062.8
Market Share Required	4.1%	3.8%	3.2%	3.2%	3.2%
Capacity Utilization	32.0%	34.0%	36.0%	38.0%	41.0%

COMPLETE SUPPLY

Financial Ratios (in thousands)	Actual					Projected		
	1980	1981	1982	1983	1984	1985		
Total Sales	2987	3268	3302	3665	4105	4639		
Current Assets	282	285	288	319	357	403		
Current Liabilities	32	33	33	37	41	46		
Current Assets Minus Current Liabilities	250	252	255	282	316	357		
Ratio of Current Assets Divided by Current Liab.	8.8	8.6	8.7	8.6	8.7	8.8		
Quick Ratio	1.0	1.0	1.0	1.0	1.0	1.0		
Total Sales Divided by the Total of Current Assets Minus Current Liabilities	12.0	13.0	13.0	13.0	13.0	13.0		
Total Liabilities	1136	1024	911	802	693	585		
Net Worth	465	467	470	498	531	572		
Total Liabilities Divided by Net Worth	2.4	2.2	1.9	1.6	1.3	1.0		

COMPLETE SUPPLY

Financial Ratios (in thousands)	Actual			Projected		
	1980	1981	1982	1983	1984	1985
[1]Net Income [2]Return on Investment	4.0/465 = 0.9%	19.9/467 = 4.3%	26.8/470 = 5.7%	28.6/498 = 5.7%	4.97/531 = 9.4%	74.7/572 = 13.1%
Cash Flow Return on Investment	117.0/465 = 25.2%	132.9/467 = 28.5%	139.8/470 = 29.7%	141.6/498 = 28.4%	162.7/531 = 30.6%	187.7/572 = 32.8%
Accounts Receivable						
Days Receivables Outstanding	3.7	3.4	3.4	3.4	3.4	3.4
Accounts Payable						
Days Payable	5.3	4.9	4.9	4.9	4.9	4.9
Inventory						
Days Inventory on Hand	40.6	37.4	37.4	37.4	37.4	37.4
Inventory Return Experience as a % of sales volume returned	1%	1%	1%			

[1]Yearend Net Income/Yearend Net Worth = Net Income Return on Investment
[2]Yearend Cash Flow/Yearend Net Worth = Cash Flow Return on Investment

COMPLETE SUPPLY

Age of Inventory @ 12/31/82

	0–30 days	31–60 days	61–90 days	90+
$ value of inventory	$74,000	$100,000	$76,000	$4,000
% of total inventory	29%	39.5%	30%	1.5%

Value of Fixed Assets @ 12/31/82

Equipment	Age	Cost	Replacement Cost	Book Value	Orderly Liquidation Value	Liens/Mortgages
Warehouse and Associated Equipment	30	$2,825	$3,500	$1,100	$2,500	878

Expenditures for Advertising, Promotion, Capital Expenditures and Development Costs

	Actual			Projected		
	1980	1981	1982	1983	1984	1985
Advertising and Promotions	$15	$17.5	$17.5	$18.7	$19.1	$19.2

Because of the nature of Complete Supply's business, the company has budgeted a negligible amount for capital expenditures.

BUSINESS PLAN FOR

Microland

a full service retail computer store

1221 W. Touhy Ave.
Skokie, Ill 60078
312-555-4321

July 1, 1982

OVERVIEW

Microland is a start-up venture that will sell and service microprocessor-based personal computer systems for business applications. Unlike the various computer retail outlets now in existence, we will focus specifically on the needs of business customers. In addition to selling a variety of microcomputer systems and peripherals, Microland will provide its customers consulting services unlike those of many other stores: custom software preparation, training seminars, and—most importantly—expert assistance in guiding business users to the best systems for their needs.

The principal competitive factors that differentiate one computer outlet from another include the following: price of products, the breadth of product lines carried, customer's waiting time for product delivery, the availability of timely service, and the technical and marketing skills of both sales and service personnel.

All these factors are important. But Microland's management thinks the last factor—the quality of personnel—is crucial to the success of a computer retail business. We plan to have a highly skilled and motivated group of employees that will set it apart from most competitors in the industry (see Training and Development).

Microland will sell computer systems made by a variety of manufacturers, including Orange Computer, IXB, Oswald Computer Corporation, Vistacorp, MiniPro, and others. Orange Computer and IXB are two major manufacturers of microcomputer hardware. Drawing on their strong financial resources and brand name awareness, both manufacturers have made a strong commitment to developing more powerful and less expensive personal computers especially tailored to business applications. Oswald Computer Corp. is strong in the portable business microcomputer market, while Vistacorp and MiniPro are the acknowledged leaders among software developers for business applications. Using computer components developed by these and other manufacturers, Microland will assemble personal computer systems to serve the business applications market.

The typical computer system will retail for $4000, and it will be used in the business setting to enhance productivity by reducing clerical time and by delivering accurate and timely information to key business decision makers. The business applications market has been extremely receptive to the productivity improvements offered by microcomputers, and this segment of the market has been growing at an annual rate of 60% for the last three years.*

The three principals of Microland—Mr. Bill Schneider, Ms. Karen Tornquist, and Mr. Mark Davis—are a strong management team. Mr. Schneider, who will serve as president and sales manager, has an engineering and business background and will be responsible for day-to-day management of our company. Ms. Tornquist, an MBA and CPA, will be responsible for the company's financial operations. Mr. Davis has experience directing the service department of a computer retail operation, and will handle that function with Microland (see Management).

As of September 15, 1982, Microland has been in the start-up planning phase. The management requires $200,000 to finance the opening of its first retail outlet in January 1983. These funds will be used for working capital, to acquire inventory, and to make necessary leasehold improvements. Two of the principals will contribute $20,000 in equity capital. To acquire the remaining $180,000, our management is offering investors a $100,000 debenture and 40% of the company's stock (see Investment Criteria). According to projections based on industry research management expects annual sales growth to exceed 120% between 1983 and 1985.

*Computers Illustrated, July 1982, "The Business Personal Computer."

STRATEGIC PLAN

Microland will serve an important market segment by concentrating specifically on the business uses of the personal computer. Thus our primary customers will be the small business owner, corporate mid-level executives, and professionals. In these markets, justifying the cost of computers is of paramount importance in making the sale. Backed by a sound understanding of business concepts, the sales and service force will be trained to understand the corporate executive's fear of computers and to bridge the gap between the world of business and the rapidly changing technical world of computing.

Although most computer stores leave this kind of marketing training to the "school of experience" and to occasional manufacturer-sponsored training programs, Microland will invest heavily in developing an in-house training program teaching both technical and marketing concepts. In this manner, there will be a free flow of information between the sales staff, the service staff, and the software development staff. An added bonus of such training will be the opportunity to evaluate new and competitive business products, thus insuring against the possibility of rapid obsolesence of our present planned product lines. Furthermore, we will be negotiating price protection and inventory buy-back agreements wherever possible. These practices, as standards in the retail industry, protect the individual stores from the sudden unfavorable price changes and technological changes that are so prevalent in the industry.

As the company grows and prospers, our highly trained business-oriented personnel will prove to be a formidable competitive edge. To protect against raids on our personnel from larger and better financed competitors, management has devised a profit-sharing plan and an employee stock purchase plan that provide unusually strong long-term loyalty incentives. Furthermore, all key employees of Microland signed five-year employment contracts as well as a protection-of-trade-secrets covenant.

In examining the probable demand for business personal computer systems, one must first determine whether the primary product benefit—an increase in productivity—is cost justified. The typical generic computer system consists of:

1. Microcomputer: microprocessor, memory, and keyboard.
2. Console Screen: black and white or green phosphor.
3. Two disk drives: usually 5.25 inch floppy drives.
4. Letter quality printer: prints type identical to that of a typewriter.

5. Accounting software: general ledger with payroll, accounts receivables/payables, and inventory.
6. Word processing software: used to produce documents, single letters, and form letters.
7. Spread sheet software: used for financial analysis, sales forecasting, production scheduling, and sensitivity analysis.

Through a generic system of this type, which retails for about $4000, the small business owner can eliminate approximately one-half of his accountant's time bill and approximately one-half of his secretarial load. On the average, he can eliminate or redeploy approximately $8400 per year. Furthermore, the intangible benefits of being able to do his own sales forecasting and of being able to inspect timely accounting data immediately are invaluable. Consequently, the personal computer is a very cost-effective tool in the business world.

Presently, the personal computer industry sells an annual volume of $2 billion. Still in its infancy, the market is barely 5% saturated. By 1985, the industry will top an annual sales volume of $5 billion. While the business markets represent over 65% of those revenues, according to Byte Market Research, Houston, most business customers are forced to hunt for information on this valuable business tool amid the squeals of children playing video games. Indeed, most of the salesmen are barely past that stage themselves. Thus, Microland thinks that the business market is tremendously underserved, and we see dramatic potential in our future growth prospects by addressing this market need. According to Computer Research, a highly respected Chicago-based market research firm, the nationwide business applications microcomputer market will grow at over 60% per year for the next five years from a base of $1.3 billion.* Although not totally insulated from seasonal factors and cyclical economic conditions, the microcomputer as a business tool is completely cost justified in terms of increased productivity. Thus, Microland's revenues and profits should continue to grow at projected rates, regardless of recessionary economic conditions.

MARKET AND COMPETITION

Microland's primary competitors will be other personal computer retailers in the Chicago area. Although our company will differentiate itself as the only Chicago area retailer catering specifically to the business market, most other personal computer retailers do sell some prod-

---

Computers Illustrated, July 1982, "The Business Microcomputer."

ucts to the business market, and therefore are considered direct competitors. On that basis, there are 27 competing computer retailers in the Chicago area, with aggregate revenues of over $35 million in 1982. Over the last three years, this revenue figure has been expanding at a compound annual rate of 50%.*

Below is a list of firms that Microland's management believes to be the five largest computer retailers in the Chicago area. Because these firms are privately held—the top three are Chicago-area franchises of national companies—it is difficult to pinpoint their sales volume and market share. The figures below are approximations; they are based on estimates of store size in square feet multiplied by $1500, the typical sales volume per square foot for computer retail stores. Market share figures are generated using the $35 million aggregate revenues figure.

Firm	No. of Stores, Total sq. ft.	Est. Revenues in 1982	Market Share
World of Computers	5 stores, 5000 sq. ft.	$7.5 million	21%
Customer's Computers	3 stores, 3330 sq. ft.	$4.995 million	14%
K World	2 stores, 2400 sq. ft.	$3.6 million	10%
CompBusiness	2 stores, 2000 sq. ft.	$3.0 million	9%
Computer Enterprise	1 store, 1500 sq. ft.	$2.25 million	6%

Microland's management thinks the estimated sales revenues for World of Computers and Customer's Computers are probably high. Both opened two additional franchises, each in the second quarter of 1982 (those new outlets are counted in the listing above), so it is unlikely those stores contributed $1500 per square foot to total revenues in 1982.

The firms listed above are formidable competitors. However, none has differentiated itself as a retail firm catering specifically to the business applications market. The firms listed above do not have custom software development expertise in-house; there is no indication that they intend to acquire such expertise. And although the World of Computers has established a positive reputation as a store with a varied stock at low prices, it has also acquired a negative reputation as an operation incapable of providing effective after-sales service. Accord-

* "Crain's Chicago Business," August 15, 1982.

ing to a survey done by two computer clubs in the Chicago area—the Orange Computer Group and the Chicago Oswald Group (COG)—World of Computers ranks as the worst dealer among the five listed above for providing after-sales service.

These top five stores also suffer from one of the major shortcomings of the computer industry—lack of qualified sales personnel. Microland's management visited all the outlets of the top five computer stores. Pretending to be customers, our management asked many questions about the various kinds of computers available and their capabilities. In many cases, salespeople had only rudimentary knowledge of what a computer could do. Computer Enterprise had the most knowledgeable people, but even they failed to explain fully the capabilities of standard software packages.

At this point, the five largest retailers have captured over 60% of the market. However, the market should expand so rapidly that there should be market opportunities for our company.

The mail order and nontraditional computer outlets are not directly competing with Microland since they serve the more price-sensitive hobbyist/home computer market. Our primary market segment will be the small business owner with revenues of under $10 million. These customers, along with professionals such as doctors and lawyers, are far more concerned with service and support considerations than with price. The primary marketing considerations are to provide timely and convenient repair service, since the loss of the computer can cripple a small business, and to provide expert consultation in evaluating computer systems to match each business customer's unique needs.

Thus, Microland's direct competitors are other Chicago-area computer retailers that service the business applications microcomputer market. In order to quantify this market, it is assumed that the business market in Chicago constitutes 65% of the total Chicago area microcomputer market, and is growing at a 60% compounded annual rate, as is true nationwide.* Thus, the business applications market in Chicago is 65% × $35 million = $22.75 million in 1982. From this business applications market, Microland projects merchandise and service revenues of $1.1 million in 1983, $1.975 million in 1984, and $5.3 million in 1985. If the business applications market grows at a 60% annual compounded rate, then the market should be $36.4 million in 1983, $58.24 million in 1984, and $93.18 million in 1985. Thus our market share is projected to be 3% in 1983, 3.39% in 1984, and 5.69% in 1985. The increasing market share projections are predicated upon the opening of two new retail stores in 1985, and the increasing importance of

* *Computers Illustrated*, July 1982, "The Business Personal Computer."

Microland's competitive edge—the Training and Development program (see Training and Development). In addition, customer software development will contribute to the growth in revenues (see Assumptions for Projected Income Statement).

Microland will initially attract business to the retail showroom primarily through advertisements in the business section of various local newspapers. These advertisements will be financed primarily through manufacturer coop funds.* Thus, the initial customers will be small business owners and professionals. These customers will also be initially garnered through catalog mailings using rented customer lists. Initially, the computer literacy seminars will be conducted free of charge, to promote awareness of Microland as a new microcomputer store oriented to business applications.

As revenues grow, and we compile our own customer lists, the company will also begin mailings and advertisements in vertical publications aimed at selected target segment such as doctors or lawyers. Establishing a reputation as a specialist serving the local professional community's business interests will aid immensely in tapping this vastly neglected segment of the business applications computer market.

In addition, the increasing importance of custom-written software, developed exactly to meet a particular business customer's needs, will continue to fuel the company's growth. In early 1985, the opening of two more retail stores will dramatically enhance this growth. Retail computer stores usually sell $1500 of computer merchandise per square foot per year. Microland will initially begin operations with one retail store with 2000 square feet of showroom space. With the opening of two new stores in 1985, this space will be tripled, paving the way for vastly increased revenues.

Our customers will be primarily professionals or small business owners with revenues under $10 million. The company will extend terms of 2% in 10 days or net 30 days to good credit risks. In addition, Microland will work through a leasing company to provide leased computer power to customers wishing to test systems and wishing to conserve cash flow.

To monitor changes in its market and customer base, our management will keep in constant contact with its customer base through service contracts and after-sale training support. In addition, Microland will monitor the pulse of the microcomputer industry through attendance at trade shows and manufacturer-sponsored seminars.

---

*"Manufacturer coop funds" means that if a retailer spends, say, one dollar of his funds for advertising, the manufacturer would match that dollar with one dollar. The ratio might be even more or less beneficial.

NEW PRODUCTS

Microland plans to develop certain software products on its own. Initially, our in-house software development staff will consist of Mr. Ken Fahey, who will be retained on a free-lance basis and compensated by Microland through sales royalties. Management believes that the custom business software market for microcomputers will yield a significant percentage of Microland's sales within three years.

Microland also plans to conduct seminars for first-time computer users in the business world. Aimed primarily at top-level corporate executives, these seminars would promote computer literacy, i.e, a thorough understanding of what computers can and cannot do in today's competitive business world. Since higher level corporate executives often feel uncomfortable with the new microcomputer technology, a tremendous demand exists for such education. Such seminars should serve as an effective marketing tool for the company. It is hoped that businessmen who participate will inform other businessmen of the usefulness of the sessions. These seminars will also enhance the image of Microland as a consultant to business users, not merely a retail outlet. While these seminars will charge students a nominal fee, they will be priced to cover the salary of the seminar leader, and not to make a short-term profit. Instead, these seminars will be used primarily to promote awareness in the market of both Microland and its product lines.

In addition, we are exploring another retail computer industry innovation, the store product catalog. Produced and mailed by Microland, this product catalog should extend the company's sales effort by reaching both new and existing personal computer sales customers in the Chicago area. These potential customers would be pinpointed using select mailing lists. Because catalogs are not widely used in the industry, no substantial evidence of their effectiveness exists. Our catalog may not prove cost effective, especially among business customers. Thus, it will be market tested on an experimental basis.

MANAGEMENT

Mr. Bill Schneider—President, Sales Manager

Ms. Karen Tornquist—Financial Vice President

Mr. Mark Davis—Service Manager

Mr. Schneider is the president and sales manager of Microland. He is 26, having been employed for three years as the sales manager of Computershop of Niles, a franchised retail computer outlet. He holds a

Bachelor of Science in Electrical Engineering from the California Institute of Technology and a Masters of Business Administration in Marketing from the Northwestern University Graduate School of Business. He has signed a five-year employment contract with Microland, contingent on the company's receiving financing. Mr. Schneider will be responsible for the day-to-day management of the company, selecting hardware and software products, conducting sales training, and conducting a marketing program to reach small business users. He will receive 20% (20,000 shares) of the common stock of Microland, but he will receive a reduced salary of $20,000 annually until the company surpasses the $500,000 mark in annual revenues. Thereafter, he will receive an annual salary of $40,000 along with bonuses from the profit sharing plan, as will all other key employees (See Profit Sharing).

Ms. Karen Tornquist is the financial vice president of Microland. She is 25, and received her MBA in finance from the University of Chicago Graduate School of Business. She also holds a Bachelor of Science degree in Accounting from the University of Chicago, and a CPA certificate. Ms. Tornquist will be responsible for financial operations and will assist Mr. Schneider in the firm's marketing efforts. She will also consult with Mr. Fahey on the development of custom-written business software. Ms. Tornquist was employed previously for two years by a big-eight public accounting firm. She will also receive 20% (20,000 shares) of the common stock of Microland, and she will be compensated on a five-year contract on the same basis as Mr. Schneider.

Mr. Mark Davis is the service manager of Microland. He is 26 and has been employed for four years as a service technician at an independent retail computer store in Lake Forest, Ill. Mr. Davis holds a Bachelor of Science Degree in Electrical Engineering from the University of Illinois, Champaign. His responsibilities will include managing the company's service department and consulting with Mr. Schneider on the selection of hardware and software. Mr. Davis will receive 5.0% (5000 shares) of the common stock of Microland, as well as a base salary of $30,000 on a five-year contract. In addition, he will receive bonuses from the profit-sharing plan.

REFERENCES References are available upon request from members of the management team.

PERSONAL OBJECTIVES

The management team at Microland is committed to providing a solid financial foundation for the company, a foundation that will help the firm participate in the rapid growth of the personal computer industry.

Catering to the business applications segment of the personal computer market, Microland will fuel its growth through the opening of additional retail outlets. The management team also plans to introduce several innovative products including computer literacy seminars, custom developed business software, and a mail order catalog. To finance these new products and to finance Microland's continued growth, management plans to take the company to the public stock market in three years.

In the future, management plans to continue the expansion of our revenues and income through a franchise program. Thus, Microland's computer literacy seminars, mail order catalog, and business-oriented training and development programs will provide the basis for inducing potential franchisees to join. Of course, great care will be taken to insure that potential franchisees meet company standards for technical and marketing expertise on an ongoing basis, in order to promote the Microland name and carefully nurtured reputation.

BOARD OF DIRECTORS

In addition to the officers of Microland, the board of directors will consist of Mr. Fahey, Mr. Rosencrans, and Mrs. Ross.

Mr. Ken Fahey will be retained by us on a free-lance basis to develop custom software packages. He will be compensated on a 20% royalty on all custom software sales, along with 2% (2500 shares) of Microland common stock. After the sale of software exceeds $250,000 annually, Mr. Fahey will be retained under a three-year contract as head of software development at a base salary of $25,000 and will receive a 10% royalty on all future custom software sales. At that point, he will also receive bonuses under the profit-sharing plan. Mr. Fahey is presently employed as a mainframe software developer at IXB, a post he has held for six years. He is 30 years old and has a Bachelor of Science in Computer Science from the University of Illinois at Champaign.

Mr. Felix Rosencrans is a senior partner at Rosencrans, Bloom and Co., a law firm with offices in Skokie, Ill. Mr. Rosencrans has been serving as a legal counsel to Microland, and has served on the board of directors of MicroDisk, a nationally known software manufacturer. He holds a Bachelor of Arts and degree in Law from Stanford University. Mr. Rosencrans is 38 years old. Mr. Rosencrans will receive 1% (1000 shares) of Microland common stock as compensation.

Mrs. Carol Ross is presently the vice president marketing for Marstton Field, a high-fashion retail department store. She has held that position for four years, before which she was employed for six years as a store manager for Marstton Field. Mrs. Ross holds a Bachelor of Arts degree from the City College of New York, and she is 40 years old. Mrs. Ross will receive 1% (1000 shares) of Microland stock as compensation.

None of the directors will receive director's fees.

REFERENCES. References from professional colleagues are available on request for members of the board of directors of Microland.

ELECTION OF THE BOARD

The common stock of Microland does not have cumulative voting rights. During the first year of operation, the Board will consist of the above six directors plus a representative of the investor group from whom financing will be obtained. In subsequent years, elections will be held during the month of February.

STRENGTHS AND WEAKNESSES OF MANAGEMENT

Mr. Schneider's primary strengths revolve around effective retail marketing. Having served three years as a sales manager at Computershop of Niles, he is extremely familiar with the computing needs of the business customer. As a sales manager, he has also had extensive experience buying computer components from a wide variety of manufacturers. He is also an excellent line manager, and he will be highly effective at training business-oriented sales forces.

While he is an excellent marketer, Mr. Schneider is not formally trained in accounting or finance. To conserve after-tax cashflow and to monitor credit terms with suppliers and customers, Ms. Tornquist was added to the management team. As a former employee of Coopers & Lybrand, Ms. Tornquist functioned as a tax consultant to small business owners, and she will add much needed financial expertise. Ms. Tornquist will also be instrumental in guiding the functional development of new custom written business software at Microland. However, Ms. Tornquist does not have the broad corporate accounting experience that would be directly related to our needs.

Mr. Davis, as the third member of management, will provide the technical expertise that is so critical to a full-service computer firm.

While he has no previous managerial experience, Mr. Davis has repaired and serviced a variety of microcomputers, and he will run an extremely effective service department for Microland.

Thus the management personnel at Microland are complementary in terms of strengths and weaknesses, and will function well to build a dynamic team. In addition, Mr. Fahey will oversee software development, while Mrs. Ross will add further retail marketing expertise. As the firm continues to prosper, more key personnel will be developed to build a broader management team. Management plans to recruit most of its future key employees from within its sales and service ranks. These individuals, because they will have experienced Microland's unique training programs, will be in the best position to assume leadership roles as the company grows. Since the total compensation levels and long-term profit incentives are highly competitive with the computer industry as a whole, Microland should be able to train and retain high caliber management personnel.

CONFLICTS OF INTEREST

Mr. Schneider, Ms. Tornquist, and Mr. Davis will all be devoting 100% of their time to the affairs of Microland. Mr. Rosencrans, retained as the legal counsel for Microland, will serve as an outside director for the company. His position as a senior partner in the law firm of Rosencrans, Bloom and Company is not expected to conflict with his Microland activities. Mrs. Ross, serving as second outside director, is employed as the vice president of marketing for Marstton Field, a high-fashion retail department store. Microland will be drawing extensively on Mrs. Ross's general retail marketing expertise. Currently, there are no conflicting business affairs between the department store and Microland. A conflict of interest could arise if Marstton Field chose to sell business computer systems, as other mass merchandisers (such as Sears Roebuck) have done. But because Marstton Field caters largely to the consumer needs of an up-scale market, it's unlikely that the store would alter its market strategy and sell business products.

The only relationship that could currently create a conflict of interest is that between Microland and Mr. Fahey. Mr. Fahey, retained as a free-lance software developer for our company, will also serve as a director for Microland, even though he is presently employed by IXB. Since IXB is a major computer manufacturer, and since Microland is planning to become a retail supplier of IXB's personal computer, there exists a potential conflict of interest. (see Legal). To accommodate this potential problem, Mr. Fahey has signed an agreement with Microland whereby he will terminate his employment with IXB and work exclusively for our company when the sale of custom business software exceeds $250,000 annually. At that point, software sales revenue will support the costs of employing Mr. Fahey, and such software will be of sufficient importance to Microland to warrant Mr. Fahey's break from the IXB organization.

PROFESSIONAL SUPPORT

Microland will use the law firm of Rosencrans, Bloom & Co., a 12-year-old corporate law firm with offices in Skokie, Ill. Microland will use the First National Bank of Chicago for all banking services. In addition, the company will use the big-eight accounting firm of Coopers & Lybrand, retaining the services of senior partner, Mr. Jack Lyons. From Mr. Lyons, we will receive professional tax consulting services as well as auditing services. In return, Mr. Lyons will receive 1% (1000 shares) of Microland common stock. Through this practice of using equity to pay for professional services, management hopes to conserve early cash flow, thereby channeling such cash flow into tangible assets necessary for continued growth. Also, by compensating its professionals with Microland common stock, management hopes to guarantee their full involvement in company matters.

OWNERSHIP

Microland will initially be capitalized with 100,000 shares of common stock.

Mr. Schneider will invest $10,000 in exchange for 20% (20,000 shares) of the common stock of Microland. He will sign a five-year employment contract as the president.

Ms. Tornquist will invest $10,000 in exchange for 20% (20,000 shares) of the common stock of Microland. She will sign a five-year employment contract as the vice president.

Mr. Davis will receive 5% (5000 shares) of the common stock of Microland. He will sign a five-year employment contract as the service manager.

Mr. Fahey will own 2.0% (2000 shares) of the common stock of Microland in return for his services as a free-lance custom software developer for us.

Mr. Rosencrans, Mrs. Ross, and Mr. Lyons will each receive 1% (1000 shares) of Microland's common stock in exchange for various professional services.

Ten percent (10,000 shares) of the common stock of Microland will be set aside for the Employee Stock Purchase Plan to encourage employees to acquire a proprietary interest in the company. In the opinion of management, such a plan will be of long-term benefit to both the employees and the shareholders because it will help Microland retain the best performing employees and lure talented newcomers.

The investors from whom Microland receives financing will be issued 40% (40,000 shares) common stock. In return, the investors will provide $80,000 in the form of an equity infusion. The investors will also provide a $100,000 debenture, to be repaid at the end of a five-year period (ending January 1988) with a 12% coupon payment due semiannually.

All common stock issued by Microland will be protected against dilution by preemptive rights. If the sales projections prove to be accurate, the next round of financing will take place in 1985 through the public stock market in order to finance the opening of two new retail outlets. At that point, Microland will raise $300,000 by issuing 25,000 additional shares at approximately $12 per share. Thus, if the present shareholders choose not to exercise their preemptive rights, they will undergo a 20% dilution of their ownership position while gaining from the company's added liquidity via proceeds from the public stock offering.

INVESTMENT CRITERIA

Microland is offering 40% (40,000 shares) of its common stock in exchange for $80,000 in equity and a $100,000 debenture with a 12% coupon rate and a five-year balloon payment. This debenture will *not* be convertible to common stock. Other investment criteria include:

1. No additional debt shall be issued without express written permission from the debenture holders.
2. No long-term capital leases will be committed to the company without express written permission of the debenture holders.
3. After the first year of operation, Microland must earn income before interest and taxes of at least three times interest charges under the debenture.
4. Dividends will not be declared by the company until bondholders receive full prepayment of principal plus interest.

5. If Microland wishes to prepay the debenture, it will also pay a penalty equivalent to 5% of the $100,000 principal.

After the financing is completed, 10% (10,000 shares) of Microland's authorized common stock will be held in reserve for the Employee Stock Purchase Plan.

The list below summarizes how the authorized shares of Microland will be distributed:

Investors	40,000 shares	40%
Mr. Schneider	20,000 shares	20%
Ms. Tornquist	20,000 shares	20%
Mr. Davis	5,000 shares	5%
Mr. Fahey	2,000 shares	2%
Mr. Rosencrans	1,000 shares	1%
Mrs. Ross	1,000 shares	1%
Mr. Lyons	1,000 shares	1%
Employee Stock Purchase Plan	10,000 shares	10%
Total	100,000 shares	100%

Both Mr. Schneider and Ms. Tornquist are willing to provide personal guarantees on the $100,000 debenture. Mr. Schneider's net worth includes equity in his house and savings totaling $52,000, while Ms. Tornquist's net worth totals $50,000.

The proceeds of the initial $180,000 raised from investors plus the $20,000 raised from Mr. Schneider and Ms. Tornquist will be used primarily to fund inventory, leasehold improvements, working capital, and start-up expenses. (See Projected Net Cash Flow chart for 1983.) As can be seen from this chart, multiple takedowns are feasible, whereby investors can withhold part of the $180,000 until late in 1983, after certain performance criteria are met. Thus the downside risk to investors is somewhat reduced and the rate of return will be increased.

LIQUIDITY

Until 1985, the shares of Microland will not be registered with the SEC and, accordingly, there will not be a public market for its common stock. If Microland shareholders wish to sell any portion of their holdings, they must seek permission of the board of directors; they must comply with highly restrictive securities regulations; and they must offer shareholders the right of first refusal. Until the company goes public, its shares will bear a legend restricting trade.

RISK FACTORS

Investment in Microland should only be made for the purpose of long-term capital gains and should be evaluated on the same terms as any other speculative business investment. As a new business enterprise, the company will face many competitive risks that could cause eventual financial failure. Some of the risk factors to be evaluated include:

1. Local competition among Chicago-area computer retailers could increase dramatically. If the number of retail outlets were to double suddenly, pricing could become the dominant competitive factor differentiating the outlets, and retail profit margins would then drop precipitously. At that point, the full-service computer stores like ours would have difficulty covering their costs of maintaining skilled personnel, further reinforcing the trend that would make pricing the dominant competitive factor among retail computer stores. Thus Microland must strive to create and maintain a distinct identity as a full-service, business-only personal computer outlet.

2. A similar competitive scenario could unfold if a large number of nontraditional retail stores started carrying computer product lines. If traditional discount chains like K Mart began selling business application computers, there would be more competitive price pressure on full-service computer stores offering wide-ranging computer literacy seminars and timely repair service. Since our primary customers will be businessmen, who will be using the more sophisticated computers as business tools, Microland should be less vulnerable to such price pressures than the computer stores selling primarily to the home consumer market. The business market will need and pay for the full service characteristics of our company.

3. Microland is more vulnerable to another form of competition in the business applications personal computer market. As the personal computer industry matures, the more sophisticated manufacturers are fielding direct sales forces to penetrate the high-volume corporate market directly. If this should occur, the company would face direct competition from its own suppliers, e.g., Orange Computer and IXB. Since these suppliers have an obvious price advantage and since they can provide superior repair or replacement services through their larger financial resources, Microland must offer a unique service that is not

available from the manufacturers. Thus, we will penetrate the corporate markets by functioning as a "systems house," designing an ideal computer component system for each client, with equipment from a variety of suppliers. Microland will provide advice and consultation—as well as computer hardware and software products—to the business client. Thus our company would have the advantage of far more consumer credibility than the captive manufacturers' sales force that can sell only one or two computer makes. Furthermore, the manufacturers do not have the expertise or financial resources to sell the low margin personal computer directly to all but the highest volume Fortune 500 customers. In fact, they have an incentive to work through us to sell to the lower volume small business markets that will be the company's primary niche.

4. Microland is also vulnerable to being completely cut off by a major supplier. Since the standard agreement in the retail computer industry can be terminated by either party in 30 days, suppliers are not obligated to continue to use this company as a retail sales outlet. Thus, we are vulnerable to changes in the distribution methods used by IXB and Orange Computer, two major manufacturers that could discontinue their use of independent retail stores and open their own captive outlets. However, neither Orange nor IXB has the expertise to maintain captive retail outlets, and they have strong cost incentives to continue using stores like Microland.

5. Microland also faces the usual risks not unique to the computer industry. Some of these risks include a sudden obsolescence of existing inventory, a dramatic slowdown in accounts receivable, or the theft of valuable inventory. Through the use of prudent business practices such as inventory buy-back contracts with suppliers, monitoring of accounts receivables and payables, profit sharing for employees, and insurance contracts, we hope to avoid such problems.

6. The shares of Microland will not be registered with the SEC until 1985. Thus, they will bear a legend restricting trade. In addition, any parties desiring to sell any shares must give the other stockholders the right of first refusal. Thus, liquidity in these shares is substantially limited.

7. Microland is also vulnerable to competition from other nontraditional computer retailers such a video and stereo houses and from mail-order outlets. As with the other competitive scenarios, if these new outlets became significantly dominant, full-service pricing might come under severe pressure and margins would deteriorate. Our management believes that the technical expertise in video/audio components is not significantly transferable to computer hardware or software; consequently, the sales staffs at stereo and video stores would be

at a disadvantage compared to the highly trained staff at Microland. Among the mail order firms, any computer expertise is unnecessary, since they attract customers solely on the basis of low prices and fast delivery. With this strategy, mail order firms could potentially hurt the sales of full-service firms like ours. Fortunately, the major computer hardware manufacturers have recognized the necessity of supporting the full-service retail outlets that provide the technical expertise in choosing and repairing computer equipment. Thus, many manufacturers have refused to sell equipment directly to the mail order houses, thereby erasing the price advantages of those outlets. In addition, Microland will serve only the business applications markets which are far less price sensitive and willing to pay for more support and service than the hobbyist/home computer market.

8. Certain competing retail chains have far more financial resources than Microland. For instance, the 150-store World of Computers franchise operation has historically enjoyed greater buying power and consumer recognition than smaller independent retail computer outlets. With pooled economies of scale in advertising and purchasing, these larger competitors could potentially reduce the viability of smaller independent outlets like ours. But major computer manufacturers have begun to recognize that not every store in a particular franchise posseses the knowledge and expertise necessary to sell their product. Recently, for instance, Orange Computer has withdrawn its recognition of World of Computers franchise system as a single network, and will only supply product to each store individually. In addition, both IXB and Orange have extended manufacturer-sponsored coop funds that defray 50% of the costs of individual store advertising. Both of these factors tend to mitigate any advantages the larger chains have, and Microland is fully confident that the growth in the personal computer industry will support both the large and small full-service outlets.

9. Microland is subject to the minimal credit terms made available to start-up retail computer stores. Without an established track record, we must give suppliers a first lien on merchandise inventory. Terms will be net 30. In the event of bankruptcy, the suppliers are entitled to recover all their inventory, on which they can expect to receive $0.80 per dollar of cost. After six months of profitable operation, these liens will be removed, and Microland will operate on standard net 20 credit terms from suppliers.

10. Microland's investors are subject to immediate dilution of their investment since they will be investing $80,000 for 40% of the company's stock in addition to the purchase of a $100,000 debenture. In contrast, the principals will invest only $20,000 in return for 50% of the

company's stock. While the $100,000 bond will be personally guaranteed by Mr. Schneider and Ms. Tornquist, the $80,000 is entirely at risk. Thus, investors bear a disproportionate share of the risk for a smaller share of the rewards. These risks will be somewhat mitigated by the multiple takedown schedule contingent on performance. And, over time, the sweat equity and management expertise provided by the principals will prove to be a significant contribution to the overall value of Microland's common stock.

11. Finally, investors should be aware that Microland's management team has no previous track record in new venture start-ups. Naturally, management will be looking for guidance not only from the company's board of directors, but also from its investors.

SIGNIFICANT COSTS

The company's most significant costs are labor and the cost-of-goods-sold. Labor costs will be held in check by providing a comprehensive training program (See Training and Development), and a compensation package tied to performance. Cost of goods sold will be minimized through the diversification of qualified suppliers.

CUSTOMER CREDIT SCREENING PROCEDURES

All credit customers must undergo the following screen before their credit is approved.

1. Reference from the customer's bank of account.
2. Credit check with the Retail Credit Association.
3. Credit check with Dun & Bradstreet Reports.

If a customer's account is not paid within 30 days of the invoice date, interest charges will accrue at an 18% annual percentage rate. After 60 days, the customer will be prohibited from charging additional merchandise against his account. After 90 days, the account will be turned over to the company's attorneys for collection.

SEASONALITY

As with most retailers, Microland's volume is expected to increase during the Christmas season and slacken during the first quarter of the calendar year. However, due to the company's "business orientation," volume is expected to be relatively evenly distributed throughout the year.

EMPLOYEES

Employee Stock Purchase Plan

Microland will adopt an Employee Stock Purchase Plan to encourage both current and future employees to acquire an ownership interest in the company. The board of directors may select participants in the plan from time to time among persons employed in an executive, professional, or supervisory capacity. No one may participate unless selected by the board, and the board will establish the criteria for selection.

Microland will make its shares available from the pool of common stock set aside for that purpose and from reacquired shares. Our company will pay all costs of administering the plan

The shares will be sold at a price (probably below market value) determined by the board of directors. Employees will pay for the stock in four equal annual installments, beginning one year from the date of the award. Installments may be prepaid. The shares will be held in escrow and released pro rata to the purchaser as each installment is paid. The shares will be sold for investment purposes only, pursuant to an exemption under the Securities Act of 1933, as amended, and the freedom of the purchaser to resell the shares will be limited accordingly.

Under the provisions of the Internal Revenue Code, a purchase of shares under the Plan at below market price will constitute a bargain purchase, and the purchaser will realize ordinary income in the year of purchase equal to the difference between the purchase price and the market price on the purchase date. Microland will be entitled to a corresponding tax deduction. The shares will then have a cost basis equal to their market price on the purchase date, and upon their disposition the purchaser will realize a capital gain or loss equal to the difference between his sale price and the market price on the date of purchase. Applicable provisions of the Internal Revenue Code may be changed in the future, and no assurance can be given as to what extent purchases of the plan may be affected.

Employee Profit Sharing Plan

Microland will institute an Employee Profit Sharing Plan that will call for 5% of the net operating profits to be distributed monthly to all employees based on their salary levels. The Profit Sharing Plan also calls for a second 5% of net operating profits to be held in trust for employees. The employees will gain vested rights to the trust after a 10-year period of employment. Thus, an employee leaving the company after two years of service will forfeit all rights to the amount held in trust for him. His portion of the trust would revert to the general pool.

Employee Compensation

Sales employees will be paid at a minimum starting salary of $4.00 per hour plus commissions and other benefits. Commissions will consist of 5% of revenues generated monthly by the employee. This commission will only be paid if the sales revenue is at least 85% of the manufacturer's suggested retail price for those items. Past experience suggests that full-time sales employees with more than one month of training will generate an average monthly sales volume of $24,000—six systems sales at an average of $4,000 each. Before profit sharing and other benefits are taken into account, the average sales employee will earn approximately $11 per hour during his first year, versus the industry average of $9 per hour.*

Service employees will be paid minimum starting salary of $20,000 per year plus profit sharing and other benefits. The service manager will receive $30,000 annually plus profit sharing and benefits. (The March 1982 issues of *Computer Age* magazine estimates that these salary levels are average for the industry.) Employees responsible for developing software will be compensated primarily through sales royalties until associated sales revenues exceed $250,000 annually. This practice is standard for the software industry. Shipping and clerical employees will be compensated at somewhat lower salary levels, approximately $15,000 per year.

In addition to their base salaries and commission structures, all employees will receive further compensation through the Profit Sharing Plan and the Employee Stock Purchase Plan. These benefits are designed to encourage valued employees to remain with the company on a long-term basis. All full-time employees will be eligible for two weeks of paid vacation annually, and all full-time employees will be eligible to buy any of Microland's products at cost. As the company's profitability increases, certain pension plans, medical insurance, and other benefits will be made available to employees who meet minimum length-of-

---

* *Salesman's Monthly Magazine*, "What you should be earning," June 1982.

service requirements. Finally, the salaries and benefits of key personnel will be raised according to specific performance criteria.

TRAINING AND DEVELOPMENT

Microland's training and development program will play a key role in the company's overall marketing strategy. We will seek to serve an important but neglected segment of the personal computer market by concentrating on the business user. To sell computers to business users our sales staff must persuade customers that the systems it carries are cost effective. Microland's sales and service personnel will be trained to explain how computers will save business users time and money. They will be taught to understand the executive's fear of computers, and to bridge the gap between the world of business and the rapidly changing and highly technical world of computers.

Microland's management has developed two intensive in-house employee training and development programs; one for sales personnel, and one for service personnel. The sales training program will teach the sales force how to operate all the product lines we carry. This program will also develop the marketing skills—analyzing a customer's needs through an awareness of business concepts—that are crucial to selling to our customers. Sales employees will receive further training in the basics of good salesmanship: qualifying and listening to the customer, closing the sale, and following through on customer needs after the sale. Besides attending Microland's in-house service training programs, service employees will attend manufacturer-sponsored technical seminars. They will then be required to brief our other employees on the information they have acquired. Experienced sales personnel will be required to conduct various seminars on selected general marketing topics and on specific products. Overall, this training program will facilitate the free flow of information between the sales staff, the service staff, and the software development staff.

Management believes that our training program will develop a technically skilled sales and service staff, who will prove highly effective in marketing personal computer systems to the business world.

PROJECTED EMPLOYEE NEEDS

The following table is a projection of future employee needs for Microland. The table assumes the validity of the sales projections shown in the pro forma income statement. It also assumes that two new stores will be opened in 1985.

EMPLOYEE NEEDS

	1983	1984	1985
Full-time	6	8	23
Part-time	3	4	4
Total	9	12	27
Seminars	2	2	2
Sales	5	5	16
Service	1	2	4
Software development	1	1	1
Clerical	0	1	2
Administrative	0	1	2
Total	9	12	27

LABOR RELATIONS

None of Microland's present employees is the subject of collective bargaining agreements between the company and a labor organization. Such agreements are rare in the retail computer industry, and management does not anticipate any labor relations difficulties. Management also believes that an adequate labor pool possessing technical and sales skills exists in the Chicago area. The area has several outstanding engineering and business schools, including Northwestern University, the University of Chicago, and the Illinois Institute of Technology. These educational institutions should insure a steady supply of intelligent and motivated personnel.

Given the existence of such a pool of intelligent and motivated potential employees, Microland could cut back on its labor force during slack economic periods. But because the microcomputer industry is expanding so rapidly, and because we will invest $3000 per employee (compared to an industry average of $1000), management does not foresee laying off any skilled sales or service employees. We will be cautious and selective in taking on new employees, hiring only when growth and profitability clearly indicate the need for additional personnel.

LOCATION AND INSURANCE

Presently, Microland is committed to a one-year lease for a 2500 square foot location in Skokie, Ill, contingent on obtaining financing. The Skokie area was recommended as a location by one of the company's principal suppliers, Orange Computer, because of a lack of competition in the area. Furthermore, Skokie is a high income residential community, and the home of many corporate executives and professionals. The particular store location is in a high traffic shopping mall with very favorable lease provisions. Furthermore, the store is located near Northwestern University, which will provide a steady source of intelligent and motivated full-time and part-time personnel.

After the company obtains financing, both principals will be insured by the company against death and disability. All inventory and assets will be insured for full replacement value against theft or fire. The company will also be covered by a premises' and blanket product liability policy. Upon the death of one of the principals, the company, based upon a specified formula, will use the life insurance proceeds to buy that principal's common stock.

Microland will be located at:

1021 W. Touhy Ave.
Skokie, Ill 60076
312-555-4321

LEGAL

Microland is structured as a corporation, incorporated on September 1, 1982 under the laws of the state of Illinois. The company has retained the firm of Rosencrans, Bloom, and Co. as legal counsel. Our management does not contemplate doing any overseas business in the near future. There are no lawsuits pending against Microland that management is aware of.

None of the three officers of Microland is subject to lawsuits from former employers, since none has signed any employment contracts or nondisclosure agreements. Among the other directors, only Mr. Fahey is vulnerable to lawsuit, due to the potential conflict of interest that exists between his present position with IXB and his future position with our company as the head of software development. However, as a highly respected software developer, Mr. Fahey has written permission in his IXB contract that allows him to engage in "creative outside interests." In addition, Mr. Fahey's position at IXB involves the development of business software for large mainframe computers, not the microcomputers that we will sell. Thus, in the opinion of Microland's counsel, the risk of a lawsuit is minimal.

All of Microland's contracts with equipment manufacturers are nonexclusive arrangements. They can be terminated by either party within 30 days written notice. With Orange Computer, Inc., a major manufacturer in the microcomputer market, Microland has a price protection clause whereby we will receive refunds from Orange for any price reductions applicable to inventory that Microland already has in stock. Vistacorp and MiniPro, two major software vendors, provide Microland with software update protection. Upon the release by the manufacturer of an updated version of the software, all obsolete inventory that we stock will be replaced at no cost.

PROTECTION AGAINST COMPETITION FROM FORMER EMPLOYEES

All officers of Microland have signed five-year contracts, as well as covenants not to compete. These covenants prohibit any employee from divulging trade secrets learned from our company. They also prohibit key personnel from leaving Microland to work for a competitive firm in the Chicago metropolitan area for a period of six months after termination of employment with us. These covenants are not made to prevent key personnel from leaving Microland—they are designed to prevent the loss of sensitive trade secrets such as our customer lists, computer literacy seminars, mail order catalogs, and training and development programs. Since these practices are not presently widespread in the retail personal computer industry they constitute a competitive edge, which Microland will use legal means to protect.

ASSUMPTIONS FOR THE PROJECTED INCOME STATEMENT

1. In 1983, the first retail store will be opened. In 1984, revenues will increase due to increased market awareness and trust. By 1985, the first store will achieve total revenues of $2.25 million. (This total revenue figure is generated by multiplying the area of

Microland's retail space—1500 square feet—by $1500, the typical revenue per square foot of a computer retail store, according to *Computers Illustrated*, "The Retail Store," April, 1982.) Also in 1985, the two newly opened stores will contribute $1,100,000 each to revenue.

2. Cost of goods sold is estimated at roughly 87% of merchandise sales; this is typical in the retail computer industry, according to *Computers Illustrated* magazine.

3. Advertising is budgeted at approximately 1.2% of sales in 1984 and 1985, with a lower percentage (0.8%) in 1983 to conserve cash flow. Commissions are calculated at 5% of merchandise sales. Sales salaries will be $4.00 per hour in 1983 and 1984, and $5.00 per hour in 1985. (See Projected Employee Needs). General & Administrative expense reflects the salaries of Mr. Schneider and Ms. Tornquist. In addition, a clerical shipping employee will be added in 1984.

4. Software royalties are estimated at 20% of software sales.

5. Profit sharing is calculated at 10% of net operating profit.

6. Leasehold improvements, service equipment, and legal fees will be depreciated/amortized over a 10-year straight-line life.

7. Interest expense on the 5-year, $100,000 debenture will be paid in two $6000 semiannual installments.

8. Federal and state income taxes are estimated to be 50% of income.

ASSUMPTIONS FOR PROJECTED BALANCE SHEET AND PROJECTED SOURCES AND USES OF WORKING CAPITAL

1. According to *Computers Illustrated*, the typical retail store's accounts receivable will turn over approximately 12 times per year. At Microland, most customers will be offered a 2% discount if they pay their invoice in 10 days or the net amount will be due in 30 days. Management assumes that most business customers will not take the discount. Therefore, it is assumed that the average account receivable will be collected in 35 days.

2. Merchandise inventory commonly turns over eight times per year. This translates into an average holding period of 46 days. For the purposes of preparing these projections, management conservatively assumed a 52-day inventory holding period.

3. Leasehold improvements and service repair equipment represent the company's only substantial fixed assets, since management plans to lease rather than own the company's retail outlets.
4. Accounts payable are assumed to be paid within 30 days, which is typical for the computer retail industry. However, management intends to pay the company's bills more promptly to strengthen Microland's relationship with its suppliers.
5. In order to fund the addition of two retail stores, the company hopes to raise $300,000 in equity capital during 1985.

ASSUMPTIONS FOR PROJECTED NET CASH FLOW

1. In 1983, net cash flow was calculated on a monthly basis (see chart entitled PROJECTED NET CASH FLOW, MONTH BY MONTH IN FIRST YEAR OF OPERATION). For simplicity, all revenues flow evenly through accounts receivable (i.e., without seasonal adjustments; see SEASONALITY). To account for collection lag, the preceding month's revenues will be collected during the month following sales.
2. For 1983, all leasehold improvements, legal fees, and security deposits associated with the opening of the first store will be paid before Microland opens its doors. Substantial leasehold improvements will be made in 1985 in connection with the opening of two new stores.
3. Rent, insurance, utilities and variable service and software development costs are assumed to begin before the first store opens. Most operating expenses are incurred uniformly on a monthly basis.
4. Inventory purchases will be made uniformly on a monthly basis, beginning with the end of the first month.
5. Microland's advertising program will demand a large pre-opening expenditure followed by an even month-by-month outlay.
6. Taxes will be paid quarterly.
7. Prepaid expenses will be funded prior to the opening of the first store in 1983 and the second and third stores in 1985.
8. Current liabilities defer the payment of cash and are therefore treated as a monthly source of cash for purposes of preparing these projections.
9. Profit-sharing distributions will be made during the last month of each calendar year.
10. For purposes of illustration, interest expense for the $100,000

debenture will be paid semiannually. The proceeds fom the debenture HAVE NOT been included in these projections as a source of revenue. These proceeds have been purposely omitted to demonstrate the company's specific financing needs.

11. As reflected by the projected net cash flow tables immediately following, 1983 operations yield a negative net cash flow of $144,567. Thus, the company must raise $200,000 in debt/ equity. In 1984, increased revenues lead to a smaller negative cash flow of $15,525, while 1985 reflects a negative net cash flow of $132,608 due to investments in leasehold improvements and inventory associated with the opening of the new retail outlets. It should be noted that in spite of the projected negative net cash flow in 1985, the company is expected to show a net income of $351,325. Thus a $300,000 public stock offering is necessary to finance 1985's expansion, which should position the company for a substantial cash surplus over the years 1985 to 1988.

ASSUMPTIONS FOR PROJECTED NET INCOME BREAKEVEN ANALYSIS, CASH FLOW BREAKEVEN ANALYSIS, AND PROJECTED FINANCIAL RATIOS

This analysis assumes that all fixed costs are inflexible in the short term. In actuality, discretionary costs, such as advertising and seminar production costs, as well as salary costs, can be substantially reduced on short notice (see Labor Relations). Thus, if revenues drop dramatically in 1985, the labor force and certain discretionary items can be reduced to lower the breakeven point dramatically.

Although projected fixed costs will substantially increase from 1983 through 1985, projected revenue gains will show dramatic growth. Consequently, net margin will increase from 2.7% in 1983 to 6.3% in 1985 due to certain economies of scale. In addition, working capital needs (mostly inventory) will continue to increase as revenues rise. With the addition of $300,000 of equity in 1985, the total ratio of liabilities to net worth will drop sharply from 1.4 : 1 in 1983 to 0.6 : 1 in 1985. Both the current and the quick ratios are projected at very acceptable levels throughout the three-year period. In order to lower the average age of the accounts receivable and inventory, management will employ state-of-the art monitoring systems, including computerized aging of receivables, tight screening and management of customer credit, and monthly physical inventory checks against automated records.

PROJECTED INCOME STATEMENT FOR MICROLAND

	1983	1984	1985
Revenues			
Merchandise Sales	$ 900,000	$1,650,000	$4,450,000
Service	200,000	325,000	850,000
Software Sales	—	—	200,000
Seminars	—	25,000	50,000
Total Sales	$1,100,000	$2,000,000	$5,550,000
Cost of Goods Sold			
Beginning Inventory	—	116,000	206,000
Purchases	900,000	1,530,000	4,219,000
(Ending Inventory)	(116,000)	(206,000)	(555,000)
Cost of Goods Sold	784,000	1,440,000	3,870,000
Gross Income	316,000	560,000	1,680,000
Rent, Insurance, Utilities	20,000	25,000	70,000
Advertising	9,000	25,000	65,000
Commissions	45,000	82,500	222,500
Sales Salaries	25,000	34,000	156,000
Seminars	10,000	12,000	30,000
Administrative	80,000	100,000	120,000
Service Salaries	30,000	55,000	100,000
Software Royalties	—	—	40,000
Service Variable Costs	10,000	19,500	47,000
Shipping	4,000	7,000	20,000
Operating Expenses	233,000	360,000	870,500
Net Operating Income	83,000	200,000	809,500
Profit Sharing	8,300	20,000	80,950
Depreciation & Amort	4,000	4,950	13,900
Interest Expense	12,000	12,000	12,000
Net Income Before Taxes	58,700	163,050	702,650
Income Tax	29,350	81,525	351,325
Net Income	29,350	81,525	351,325

PROJECTED BALANCE SHEET FOR MICROLAND

	1983	1984	1985
Current Assets			
Cash	$ 24,250	$ 26,575	$ 106,175
Marketable Securities	17,850	—	33,625
Accounts Receivable	105,000	180,000	530,000
Merchandise Inventory	116,000	206,000	555,000
Prepaid Expenses	10,000	10,000	30,000
Total Current Assets	273,100	422,575	1,254,800
Leasehold Improve- ments & Equipment	35,000	44,500	134,000
Less Accumulated Depreciation	(3,500)	(7,950)	(21,350)
Security Deposits	5,000	4,000	12,000
Legal Fees	5,000	5,000	5,000
Less Accumulated Amortization	(500)	(1,000)	(1,500)
Fixed Assets	41,000	44,550	128,150
Total Assets	314,100	467,125	1,382,950
Current Liabilities			
Accounts Payable	58,000	105,000	288,000
Accrued Expenses	24,750	47,750	123,750
Customer Deposits	2,000	3,500	9,000
Total Current Liabilities	84,750	156,250	420,750
Long-Term Debt	100,000	100,000	100,000
Total Liabilities	184,750	256,250	520,750
Capital Stock	100,000	100,000	400,000
Retained Earnings	29,350	110,875	462,200
Net Worth	129,350	210,875	862,200
Total Liabilities and Net Worth	314,100	467,125	1,382,950

PROJECTED SOURCES AND USES OF WORKING CAPITAL
FOR MICROLAND

	1983	1984	1985
Sources of Working Capital			
Net Income	$ 29,350	$81,525	$351,325
Depreciation/Amortization	4,000	4,950	13,900
Total Sources from Operations	33,350	86,475	365,225
5-Year Bond Issue	100,000	—	—
Equity Raised	100,000	—	300,000
Total Sources of Working Capital	233,350	86,475	665,225
Uses of Working Capital			
Leasehold Improvements & Equipment	35,000	9,500	89,500
Security Deposits	5,000	(1,000)	8,000
Legal Fees	5,000	—	—
Total Uses of Working Capital	45,000	8,500	97,500
Net Increases in Working Capital	$188,350	$77,975	$567,725
Cash	24,250	2,325	79,600
Marketable Securities	17,850	(17,850)	33,625
Accounts Receivable	105,000	75,000	350,000
Merchandise Inventory	116,000	90,000	349,000
Prepaid Expense	10,000	—	20,000
Net Increase in Current Assets	273,100	149,475	832,225
Accounts Payable	58,000	47,000	183,000
Accrued Expenses	24,750	23,000	76,000
Customer Deposits	2,000	1,500	5,500
Net Increases in Current Liabilities	84,750	71,500	264,500
Net Increases in Working Capital	$188,350	$77,975	$567,725

PROJECTED NET CASH FLOW BY MONTH FOR MICROLAND'S FIRST YEAR OF OPERATION

	Pre-Opening	One	Two	Three	Four	Five	Six	Seven	Eight	Nine	Ten	Eleven	Twelve
Uses of Cash													
Prepaid Expenses	$10,000	—	—	—	—	—	—	—	—	—	—	—	—
Leasehold Improvements & Equipment	35,000	—	—	—	—	—	—	—	—	—	—	—	—
Legal Fees	5,000	—	—	—	—	—	—	—	—	—	—	—	—
Security Deposits	5,000	—	—	—	—	—	—	—	—	—	—	—	—
Rent, Insurance, Utilities	1,667	1,667	1,666	1,667	1,667	1,666	1,667	1,667	1,666	1,667	1,667	1,666	—
Variable Service & Software Costs	833	833	834	833	833	834	833	833	834	833	833	834	834
Salaries, Commissions, & Royalties	—	15,000	15,000	15,000	15,000	15,000	15,000	15,000	15,000	15,000	15,000	15,000	15,000
Advertising	3,000	500	500	500	500	500	500	500	500	500	500	500	500
Shipping	—	333	333	334	333	333	334	333	333	334	333	333	334
Inventory Purchases	—	75,000	75,000	75,000	75,000	75,000	75,000	75,000	75,000	75,000	75,000	75,000	75,000
Seminars	833	833	833	834	833	833	834	833	833	834	833	833	834
Interest Expense	—	—	—	—	—	—	6,000	—	—	—	—	—	6,000
Profit Sharing	—	—	—	—	—	—	—	—	—	—	—	—	8,300
Income Taxes	—	—	—	7,338	—	—	7,337	—	—	7,338	—	—	7,337
Total Uses of Cash	60,500	94,166	94,166	101,506	94,166	94,166	107,505	94,166	94,166	101,506	94,166	94,166	113,305
Sources of Cash													
Revenues	—	—	91,667	91,666	91,667	91,667	91,666	91,667	91,667	91,666	91,667	91,667	91,666
Increase in Current Liabilities	—	7,063	7,062	7,063	7,062	7,063	7,062	7,063	7,062	7,063	7,062	7,063	7,062
Total Sources of Cash	—	7,063	98,729	98,729	98,729	98,730	98,728	98,730	98,729	98,729	98,729	98,730	98,728
Net Cash Flow Before Stock & Debenture Financing	(60,500)	(87,103)	4,563	(2,777)	4,563	4,564	(8,777)	4,564	4,563	(2,777)	4,563	4,564	(14,577)

PROJECTED NET CASH FLOW FOR MICROLAND

	1983	1984	1985
Uses of Cash			
Prepaid Expenses	$ 10,000	$ —	$ 20,000
Leashold Improvements & Equipment	35,000	9,500	89,500
Legal Fees	5,000	—	—
Security Deposits	5,000	(1,000)	8,000
Rent, Insurance, and Utilities	20,000	25,000	70,000
Variable Service and Software Costs	10,000	19,500	47,000
Salaries, Commissions, and Royalties	180,000	271,500	638,500
Advertising	9,000	25,000	65,000
Shipping	4,000	7,000	20,000
Inventory Purchases	900,000	1,530,000	4,219,000
Seminars	10,000	12,000	30,000
Interest Expense	12,000	12,000	12,000
Profit Sharing	8,300	20,000	80,950
Income Taxes	29,350	81,525	351,325
Total Uses of Cash	$1,237,650	$2,012,025	$5,651,275
Sources of Cash			
Revenues	$1,008,333	$1,925,000	$5,254,167
Increase in Current Liabilities	84,750	71,500	264,500
Total Sources of Cash	$1,093,083	$1,996,500	$5,518,667
Net Cash Flow Before Stock & Debenture Financing	$ (144,567)	$ (15,525)	$ (132,608)

PROJECTED NET INCOME BREAKEVEN ANALYSIS FOR MICROLAND

	1983	1984	1985
Revenues	$1,100,000	$2,000,000	$5,500,000
Variable Costs			
Cost of Goods Sold	784,000	1,440,000	3,870,000
Royalties & Commissions	45,000	82,500	262,500
Shipping	4,000	7,000	20,000
Variable Service Costs	10,000	19,500	47,000
Total Variable Costs	843,000	1,549,000	4,199,500
Fixed Costs			
Advertising[1]	9,000	25,000	65,000
Seminars[1]	10,000	12,000	30,000
Salaries[1]	135,000	189,000	376,000
Rent, Insurance, Utilities	20,000	25,000	70,000
Depreciation & Amortization	4,000	4,950	13,900
Interest	12,000	12,000	12,000
Total Fixed Costs	190,000	267,950	566,900
Breakeven Revenues[2]	$813,230	$1,188,248	$2,397,501

[1] Discretionary costs

[2] Breakeven Revenues = $\dfrac{\text{(Actual Revenues)(Fixed Costs)}}{\text{(Actual Revenues} - \text{Variable Costs)}}$

PROJECTED CASH FLOW BREAKEVEN ANALYSIS FOR MICROLAND

	1983	1984	1985
Revenues	$1,100,000	$2,000,000	$5,500,000
Variable Costs			
Cost of Goods Sold	784,000	1,440,000	3,870,000
Royalties & Commissions	45,000	82,500	262,500
Shipping	4,000	7,000	20,000
Variable Service Costs	10,000	19,500	47,000
Total Variable Costs	843,000	1,549,000	4,199,500
Fixed Costs			
Advertising[1]	9,000	25,000	65,000
Seminars[1]	10,000	12,000	30,000
Salaries[1]	135,000	189,000	376,000
Rent, Insurance, Utilities	20,000	25,000	70,000
Interest	12,000	12,000	12,000
Total Fixed Costs	186,000	263,000	553,000
Breakeven Revenues[2]	$796,109	$1,166,297	$2,338,716

[1] Discretionary costs

[2] Breakeven Revenues $= \dfrac{\text{(Actual Revenues)(Fixed Costs)}}{\text{(Actual Revenues} - \text{Variable Costs)}}$

PROJECTED FINANCIAL RATIOS FOR MICROLAND

	1983	1984	1985
Revenues	$1,100,000	$2,000,000	$5,550,000
Net Operating Income	85,000	200,000	809,500
Net Income after Taxes	29,350	81,525	351,325
Net after Tax Cash Flow	33,350	86,475	365,225
Return on Assets	9.3%	17.5%	25.4%
Return on Equity	22.6%	38.7%	40.7%
Cash Flow on Equity	25.8%	41.0%	42.4%
Gross Margin	28.7%	28.0%	30.3%
Net Margin	2.7%	4.1%	6.3%
Revenues/Assets	3.5x	4.3x	4.0x
Days Receivables Out-standing	35 days	33 days	35 days
Days Inventory on Hand	54 days	52 days	52 days
Days Payables Outstanding	27 days	27 days	27 days
Working Capital	$ 188,350	$ 266,325	$ 834,050
Working Capital/Net Worth	1.5	1.3	1.0
Revenue/Working Capital	5.8	7.5	6.6
Current Assets/Current Liabilities	3.2	2.7	3.0
Total Liabilities/Net Worth	1.4	1.2	0.6
Quick Assets/Current Liabilities	1.7	1.3	1.6
Service Costs/Revenues	3.6%	3.7%	2.6%
Advertising/Revenues	0.8%	1.3%	1.2%
Change in Gross Lease-hold Improvements & Equipment Revenues	3.2%	0.5%	1.6%
Direct Labor (including commissions)/Revenues	16.4%	13.6%	10.8%
Gross Leasehold Improve-ments & Equipment/Assets	11.1%	9.5%	9.7%

PROJECTED EXPENDITURES FOR CAPITAL EQUIPMENT, RESEARCH AND DEVELOPMENT, AND ADVERTISING FOR MICROLAND

	1983	*1984*	*1985*
Capital Expenditures (Leasehold Improvements and Equipment)	$35,000	$ 9,500	$89,500
Advertising	9,000	25,000	65,000

Note: During the first three years, the company will have no research & development expenses because the software authors will be compensated on a royalty basis, and will be responsible for software development expense.

*INDEX

*Note: Specific information about the fictitious companies described in Part Two may be found under *Complete Supply Service* and *Microland*.